ADVENTUROUS PUB WALKS
IN
KENT

Michael Easterbrook

COUNTRYSIDE BOOKS
NEWBURY BERKSHIRE

COUNTRYSIDE BOOKS
3 Catherine Road
Newbury, Berkshire

To view our complete range of books,
please visit us at
www.countrysidebooks.co.uk

ISBN 1 85306 835 7

Photographs by the author
Designed by Peter Davies, Nautilus Design

Produced through MRM Associates Ltd., Reading
Printed by J. W. Arrowsmith Ltd., Bristol

CONTENTS

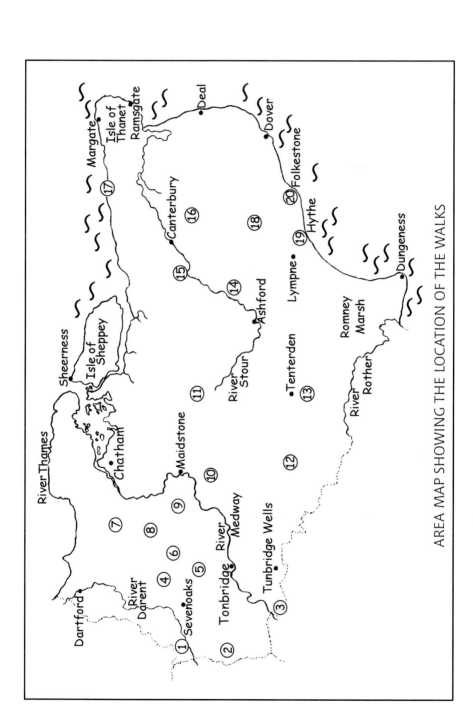

AREA MAP SHOWING THE LOCATION OF THE WALKS

ACKNOWLEDGEMENTS

I am grateful to Mike Lyth, Roy and Chris Murray, and Val, Cheryl, Craig and Jolene Easterbrook for keeping me company on various walks.

PUBLISHER'S NOTE

*W*e hope that you obtain considerable enjoyment from this book; great care has been taken in its preparation. Although at the time of publication all routes followed public rights of way or permitted paths, diversion orders can be made and permissions withdrawn.

We cannot, of course, be held responsible for such diversion orders and any inaccuracies in the text which result from these or any other changes to the routes or any damage which might result from walkers trespassing on private property. We are anxious though that all details covering the walks are kept up to date and would therefore welcome information from readers which would be relevant to future editions.

The simple sketch maps that accompany the walks in this book are based on notes made by the author whilst checking out the routes on the ground. However, for the benefit of a proper map, we do recommend that you purchase the relevant Ordnance Survey sheet covering your walk. The Ordnance Survey maps are widely available, especially through booksellers and local newsagents.

INTRODUCTION

Kent has long been known as the 'Garden of England' and, although the area of fruit growing has declined, there are still fine displays of blossom in spring. Despite its position in the crowded south-east of England, Kent has surprisingly tranquil areas away from the towns and motorways. There are over 4,000 miles of footpaths in the county, providing ample opportunity to explore this beautiful countryside, which ranges from the rolling hills of the North Downs to the Weald's woods and the marshy flatlands of Romney Marsh. Kent also has an extensive coastline and several major rivers flowing into the sea, including the Medway, Stour and Darent.

The walks in this book take you through these different types of terrain, each with its characteristic landscapes and wildlife. Several of the walks, including those from Kemsing, Cobham, Harrietsham, Wye and Elham, go over chalk downland where nature lovers can admire a tremendous variety of colourful wild flowers and butterflies in season. Woodland walks, such as those from Westerham, Cranbrook and Chilham, are particularly lovely in spring when there are carpets of bluebells, wood anemones, celandines and other flowers and the air resonates with birdsong. Birds are also a feature on the coastal section of the walk from Reculver as waders, gulls and ducks congregate on the foreshore. Another coastal walk takes you through Folkestone Warren, then up the white cliffs for superb views over the English Channel, while walks along the Greensand Ridge from Ightham Mote and Linton provide magnificent vistas over the Weald. If you enjoy waterside walks, the routes from Edenbridge and East Malling feature sections alongside rivers, with dragonflies in summer and other riverside wildlife to observe.

As well as admiring the countryside, you will discover many aspects of Kent's long history as you pass medieval, timbered hall-houses, weatherboarded cottages, fine manor houses and churches that date back to Norman or even earlier times. You will see working windmills at Cranbrook and Sarre and lovely restored watermills on the Bekesbourne walk, and you may catch nostalgic views of steam trains while walking near Groombridge or Tenterden. Other characteristic features of the Kentish landscape are the white-cowled, round-towered oast-houses, a legacy of the formerly widespread hop industry but now mostly converted to dwellings. You will follow in the footsteps of the pilgrims who flocked to Canterbury to visit Thomas â Becket's tomb and pass the castle from which his murderers left to commit their evil deed. At Cobham and Godmersham, you will tread where Charles Dickens and Jane Austen roamed.

Parts of the walks use sections of officially-designated long-distance footpaths through Kent, and if you are interested in walking these, Kent County Council has produced an excellent series of illustrated guidebooks. However, the routes also follow footpaths that are used less often and so careful navigation is required. As an aid, it is recommended that you carry the relevant Ordnance Survey Explorer map and use this in conjunction with the sketch map provided with the walk description. Some of the paths will get muddy after wet weather, so make sure you have suitable footwear. Because the walks are quite long, ranging in distance from 7½ to almost 12 miles, and may involve some strenuous climbs, a reasonable level of fitness is required. There may also be several stiles to negotiate. However, you will be rewarded with some glorious views and have the excuse to indulge in some good food.

The pubs form an integral part of the walks and have been chosen for their welcoming atmosphere and wide range of fine food and drink. They may be at the start/end of the circular walks or near the mid-point, or sometimes you have a choice of either point. If you wish to leave your car at the pub, rather than use the car park suggested, it is often possible but check with the landlord first. Many of the pubs will be busy, particularly at weekends, so it may be advisable, to book ahead for a meal, using the telephone number provided. On some walks a teashop is also available and so I also checked these out, purely in the interests of research, but thereby regaining all the calories expended on the walk! You can also help the local rural economy by purchasing other provisions at local stores and farm shops.

Information on how to get to the start of the walk is provided, as well as the location of car parks. Do check to see whether the car park closes at a particular time. Several of the walks are also accessible by public transport and details are given, with further information available on the website www.kentpublictransport.info; traveline 0870 6082608; train enquiries 08457 484950.

I hope you enjoy these longer walks and get a sense of achievement from completing them, while exploring parts of the county that may be new to you.

Michael Easterbrook

WESTERHAM, TOY'S HILL AND FRENCH STREET

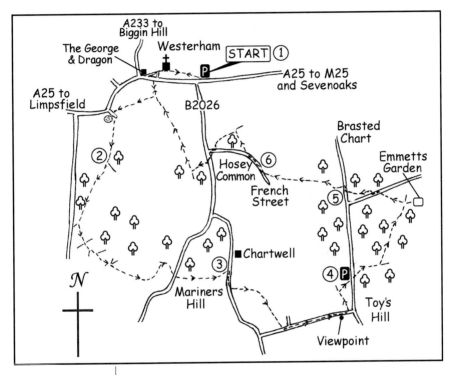

Distance:
8½ miles

Starting Point:
The public car park at Westerham, GR 450542. Alternativly, use the National Trust car park at Toy's Hill, GR 470517, and start the walk at point 4.

Map: OS Explorer 147 Sevenoaks & Tonbridge

How to get there: Westerham is at the junction of the A233 with the A25, west of Sevenoaks, with the car park on the north side of the A25, on the eastern edge of the town. There are buses from Sevenoaks and Bromley.

A MARVELLOUS VIEW TO THE NORTH DOWNS

The small town of Westerham is known for its association with several famous figures from history, including Winston Churchill and General Wolfe, and makes a pleasant start to this walk. The route takes you through the lovely heavily-wooded countryside to the south of the town. It is delightful in spring when there are carpets of bluebells, while in autumn you can admire the glorious leaf tints or revert to childhood by kicking your way through the fallen leaves. You pass Churchill's home at Chartwell and have a wonderful view from Toy's Hill across the Weald to the high ground of Ashdown Forest. There are more spectacular views as you return to Westerham, where a good selection of inns and teashops awaits you.

The **George and Dragon** enjoys a fine position in the centre of the town. It is on the high street near to the green with its statues of Churchill and General Wolfe. Indeed, it is recorded that General Wolfe stayed at the George and Dragon in 1785.

This is a Chef and Brewer pub and has a good selection of above average meals and snacks at reasonable prices. Telephone: 01959 563071.

In addition, there is also the **Tudor Rose** restaurant and tearooms which provides light meals, cream teas and a tantalising choice of delicious cakes.

Telephone: *01959 562391.*

 *The Walk*

① Leave the car park at the pedestrian exit by an information board to go on a path between houses, straight across an estate road, and through a churchyard to the green in **Westerham**. Go left across the green past the statue of Winston Churchill, cross the main road, and go up steps to an alley known as **Water Lane**. Follow this down between gardens to a gate, then turn sharp right along the right edge of a meadow to reach a lane opposite a pond. Turn left to go past a lodge house, then go right on a path (not over the stile ahead) to go uphill. The path bends left to a stile, then slightly diagonally right across a field to another. Maintain direction through a copse of trees to a stile. (1 mile)

② Go straight across the track beyond the stile, on a path into a wood and keep ahead on it, ignoring any side paths. After ¾ mile, where a track joins from the left, go over a stile by a metal gate and continue past a cottage, then 100 yards before a road seen through trees ahead turn left at a marker post. Continue through woodland and over a stony cross-track, then 50 yards on take the left fork in the path by a holly bush. Keep straight on at the next marker post, then at another 100 yards on take the right fork. At a clearing, keep ahead past a seat then turn left along a gravel drive alongside a tall cherry laurel hedge around gardens. Continue ahead as the drive becomes a track then at a fork by a marker post go left into trees and continue alongside a fence around large gardens on the right, ignoring a path going off left. At the end of the gardens turn right at a marker post and go past the gate of **April Cottage** to a road. Cross slightly to the right and go up a bridleway at **Mariners Hill**. Keep straight on at a marker post at the top of the slope and follow a wide track through trees to a road. (2 miles)

11

Chartwell – a short distance to the left here – a Victorian house with Tudor origins, was bought by Winston Churchill in 1924 and he lived there until his death in 1965. It is now owned by the National Trust and visitors can view his study, paintings and lovely garden.

③ The walk continues to the right. Take care as you walk along the road for 300 yards round a bend, then go left on a drive to **Chartwell Farm**. Keep right at the first fork and left at another 10 yards on, to go past farm buildings and ahead on a concrete track past oast-houses. Where the concrete ends go straight on through a gateway, then turn right before a metal gate onto a narrow path. This soon widens, with a wooden fence on the right, and continues between fields to a lane. Turn left, then keep straight on along the lane for ½ mile, going gradually uphill to reach **Toy's Hill** village, where there is a viewpoint by a well on the right with wonderful views over the **Weald** to **Ashdown Forest**. Continue to a T-junction, but go left at a bridleway sign 10 yards before it. After 10 yards take the left fork to go uphill on a path through trees, then 100 yards past a wooden barrier go right at a marker post for a **NT** orange walk to reach the car park at **Toy's Hill**. (1¾ miles)

THE GEORGE AND DRAGON, WESTERHAM

④ Go ahead through the car park to a road and straight across to a footpath sign and marker post for **NT** red and green walks. At another post 50 yards into the wood take the left fork (**Greensand Way (GSW)**) to reach a five-way junction of paths and continue on the **GSW** by taking the path at 2 o'clock. At the next post leave the **GSW** by going left on a cross-track. Keep straight over a cross-track, then at a second go ahead slightly to the right and gradually uphill through the wood. At the next cross-path, with yellow arrows pointing both ways, **Emmetts Garden** (with its teashop) is a short distance to the right but the walk continues to the left to reach a lane opposite **Ide Hill House**. Turn left, then at the end of the wooden fence on the right go right into trees at a **NT** horseshoe sign and bear immediately left to walk parallel to the lane, later veering right to a road. (1¼ miles)

Emmetts Garden, now in the hands of the National Trust, is renowned for the displays of rhododendrons, azaleas and bluebells in spring and also has rare trees and shrubs. If entering the garden from the walk, please go through to the kiosk to pay.

⑤ Turn right into **Brasted Chart** but after 200 yards, at the end of a row of houses, turn left on a path to the right of a track. At a T-junction with another path turn right, then at a field go left over a stile and ahead over the first part of the field to a stile in the fence on the left. Continue downhill, then over a stony cross-track to a stile and down a field to a stile and footbridge, then up steps to a lane at **French Street**. (¾ mile)

⑥ Turn right past a private cemetery with 400-year-old yew tree, then 50 yards past stone cottages keep ahead at a footpath sign as the lane starts to bend left, to go over a farm drive and along the right edge of a wood. At a T-junction with another path turn left and continue left on a tarmac drive to a lane. Turn right and just before a road junction go left across a grassy area to the small car park at **Hosey Common**. Cross the road and continue in your previous direction for 50 yards, then turn right on a path alongside a beech hedge and into trees. Turn right at a cross-track and after a section of boardwalk keep ahead right, with a large garden on the right. At the next cross-track bear right, then as the track bends left keep ahead to a stile and up the right edge of a steep field alongside tall trees. Bear slightly left to a stile, with a great view to **Westerham church** and the hills beyond, then go straight down a field to a gate and back up the alley to **Westerham**. (1¾ miles)

Date walk completed:

EDENBRIDGE AND THE EDEN VALLEY

THE OLD CROWN INN AT EDENBRIDGE DATES BACK TO THE 15TH CENTURY

Distance:
9¼ miles

Map: OS Explorer 147 Sevenoaks & Tonbridge

Starting Point:
The car park off
Croft Lane in
Edenbridge,
GR 445463.

How to get there: *Edenbridge is on the B2026,
between the A25 at Westerham and the A264. Travelling
south, turn left into Croft Lane and follow it round to the
right to the car park. Edenbridge has two railway
stations, of which Edenbridge Town is closest to the start.*

*T*he walk starts at Edenbridge, a pleasant small town with several attractive timbered buildings from the 15th century. The first part of the route follows meadows alongside the narrow, meandering River Eden before passing the site of a 14th century castle and climbing a wooded ridge where an Iron Age fort was situated. There are tremendous views over the valley to distant hills. After following the route of a Roman road, the walk continues through the Eden Valley, crossing the river to the east of Edenbridge and joining the Eden Valley Walk long-distance path to return to the town.

Ye Old Crown Inn is easily found because of its unique bridging sign over the main street in **Edenbridge**. The inn dates back to the 15th century, as indicated by the beams inside, and its long history includes its use as a haunt by a notorious gang of smugglers, with a concealed passage still in existence. Lighter meals such as chicken, smoky bacon and vegetable pie and jacket potatoes can be eaten in the spacious bar areas and Tetley's, Greene King IPA and Charles Wells Bombardier are among the ales served. There is also a separate restaurant with a good choice of fish dishes, mussels, daily roasts and old favourites like sausages and mash.

Telephone: *01732 867896.*

 *The Walk*

① Take the pedestrian exit from the car park to the main street and cross slightly left to go along **Lingfield Road**, opposite the National Westminster Bank. Keep left where the road forks after 300 yards, then after a further 300 yards turn left into **Coomb Field Road** and keep straight on to a playing field. Turn sharp left along the edge of the field to a marker post, then right along the left edge of the sports field, with trees on the left. The first part of the walk follows the long-distance **Eden Valley Walk** so you can follow the markers for it. Cross a footbridge, keep straight on across a field and over another footbridge by a pillbox, then along the left edge of a field, with the River Eden on the left, before bending right to a marker post and straight on into trees. Continue along the left edge of fields to a footbridge and stile, then straight on past another pillbox to a marker post

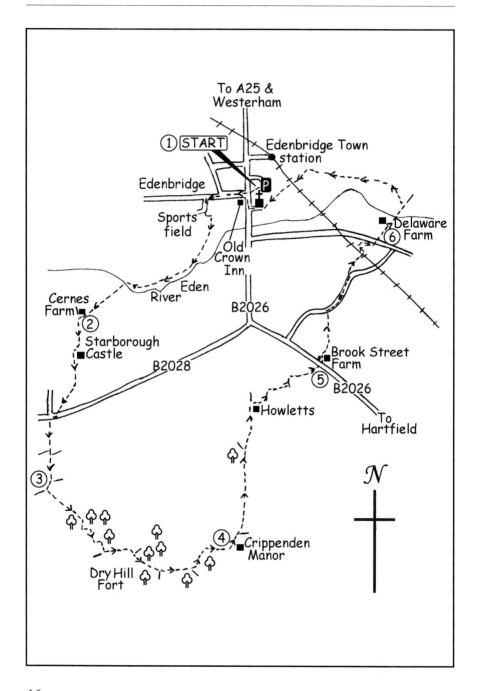

and follow the riverbank as it bends left. About 400 yards past the pillbox turn sharp left through a gap in bushes to cross a footbridge over the river, then go straight across a field and ahead on a wide sandy track through a marshy area. Keep ahead through a gateway in a fence to cross a field to a footbridge and stile near a farmhouse in trees and straight across a field to a stony track. (2 miles)

② Leave the **Eden Valley Walk** here by going left on the track, now following another long-distance path, the **Vanguard Way**. The track bends right near a large house, then 30 yards on go left over a stile and along the left edge of a field alongside a hedge and some fine oak trees.

This house was built on the site of Starborough Castle, built in the 14th century but destroyed in 1650. Only the moat remains from the castle.

After 300 yards go left over a stile then immediately right along a drive through an avenue of lime trees. Go right over a stile after 200 yards, then diagonally left, aiming for the far corner of the field. Go over a stile to a road, turn right for 40 yards and cross to a bridleway just before a house. Follow the wide track, keeping straight on at the end of the field and again at a marker post 30 yards on, to continue between hedges to a metal gate. (1¼ miles)

FINE VIEWS FROM THE HILLS NEAR EDENBRIDGE

③ Turn right on a track for 80 yards then left through another gate and gradually uphill on a narrower track between hedges, with fine views across to the **North Downs** in the left distance. Continue through a wood, then quite steeply uphill on the edge of trees, with good views behind, before bending left and right past farm buildings. Just past a house and garden at the end of the wood leave the **Vanguard Way** by going left on a cross-track. Ignore a gate on the left after 10 yards to continue on a sandy path between fences and through a gateway into a wood. After 20 yards turn right at a post to go on a wide path through conifers, with the site of **Dry Hill Iron Age fort** to the right. Look for a marker post on the left and 10 yards past it take the left fork to reach a gate as the wood opens out to the left, with terrific views. Continue along the right edge of a field to reach a metal gate into a wood. Don't go through it, but turn left along the edge of the wood, through another gate, and 300 yards on turn right into the wood at a wooden gate. Pass a pond and keep straight on through the trees to a gate, then turn sharp left before bending right to a tarmac drive. (1¾ miles)

④ Turn left along the drive and as it bends right go left at a marker post, through a metal gate to another, then along the right side of a field and straight on at the next post to a stile

in the hedge. Continue along the left edge of a succession of fields to a stile onto a tarmac drive and maintain direction along it, following the route of a Roman road. Just past a wooden barrier fence go right over a stile by the entrance to **Howletts** and along a drive to a stile by a gate. Turn sharp left past a garden, keep left of trees surrounding a pond, then bend right to a stile by a metal gate. Continue along the left edge of a small field to a stile, then the right edge of the next to a stile on the edge of trees and ahead on a path, then a drive, to a road. (1½ miles)

⑤ Cross with care and continue up a drive to a converted oast-house. At the end of the pond on the left turn left for a few yards, then right across a lawn behind a cottage to go left of a garage block and caravan and through a metal gate. Keep straight ahead across a field to a gap in a hedge and straight over another field to a footbridge, then continue on a path between fences to go past farm buildings and ahead to a lane. Turn right and continue on the lane as it bends left, ignoring footpath signs until it bends right. Here return to the **Eden Valley Walk** by going left through a green barrier and slightly diagonally left across a field and through an archway under a railway. Turn sharp left alongside the railway embankment to a marker post, then diagonally right across a field, aiming for the left of three houses. At the

THE 13TH CENTURY CHURCH AT EDENBRIDGE

stile and continue on a track to another. From here go diagonally left across a long field, keeping left of a sunken area to reach a stile to the left of a gateway in the far corner. (If you reach a kissing gate to the right of a gateway you have gone too far right and need to go left alongside the hedge for 300 yards.) Keep straight ahead across the next field, keeping left of a clump of trees, to a kissing gate in the hedgeline, then ahead to a footbridge on the left edge of trees. Continue along the right side of a field to a stile by a large oak, then ahead to a post and sharp left in front of a hedge. The path leads to a gap in the hedge and a kissing gate and on to a stony track over the railway. At an estate road, cross slightly right to go up **Churchfield**, then left into an alley at its end to enter the churchyard. The car park can be accessed through a gap in the wall on the right, otherwise continue to the main street and turn right to the pub. (1½ miles)

hedge turn right before a stile to go alongside the hedge for 150 yards and then left through a metal gate to a road. (1¼ miles)

⑥ Go straight across and along the drive to **Delaware Farm**, following it as it bends right and left and becomes a stony track that crosses a narrow section of the river. Cross a

Parts of Edenbridge church date back to Norman times, while the tower was built in the 13th century. The building material is sandstone, which looks lovely when the sun shines on it.

Date walk completed:

GROOMBRIDGE, TUNBRIDGE WELLS COMMON AND SPELDHURST

THE CROWN AT GROOMBRIDGE IS AT THE END OF A ROW OF PRETTY COTTAGES

Distance:
9½ miles

Starting Point:
The car park by the village hall at Groombridge, GR 531373.

Map: OS Explorers 18 Ashdown Forest and 147 Sevenoaks & Tonbridge

How to get there: *From the A264 take the B2110 to Groombridge and turn into Station Road. The walk could also be started from car parks near the Pantiles in Tunbridge Wells. The main line railway station in Tunbridge Wells is ¾ mile from the route (point 4).*

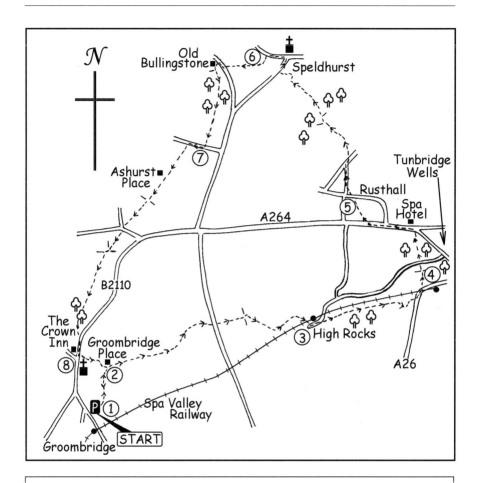

There is a wonderful start to this walk as you pass the lovely moated manor house of Groombridge Place, with a possible added bonus of glimpsing a flying display by birds of prey in the grounds. Soon you may see or hear a steam train as you walk alongside the restored Spa Valley Railway, then you pass the impressive sandstone outcrops at High Rocks. The walk continues through woodland on the outskirts of Tunbridge Wells, crosses Rusthall Common and goes into more woods around the village of Speldhurst. You pass 15th century thatched cottages and walk through pleasant parkland and farmland before reaching an ancient inn by Groombridge's picturesque green.

21

The Crown Inn is in a lovely position at the end of a row of pretty cottages above the green at Groombridge. Dating from the 17th century, it was once a den for smugglers and later a coaching inn and still makes a welcome stop for weary travellers today. There are beams, huge inglenook fireplaces and old photographs of the locality in the bars and restaurant, where you can sample local fruit juices, a good selection of wines by the glass, and Harveys Sussex pale ale, Larkins, and Greene King IPA and Abbot ales. The extensive menu includes rustic lamb and chicken cassoulet with warm ciabatta bread and chargrilled rib-eye steak, plus daily specials and bar meals such as steak and ale pie and beer battered cod. Ploughman's, jacket potatoes, crostinis and salads are also available and there is a children's menu. Outside, at the front of the inn, there are picnic tables on a sunny terrace, with fine views over the village.

Telephone: *01892 864742.*

The Walk

① From the rear of the car park at **Groombridge village hall** take a path, signed to **Groombridge Place**, that goes behind the wooden fence then bends left along the left edge of a field to a metal gate. Continue to bend left between a hedge and fence and keep alongside the fence as it bends right, to reach a stony track and keep ahead for 20 yards to cross a bridge. (¼ mile)

(If you want to visit the pub at this stage turn left here alongside the moat, then where it ends keep ahead alongside a metal fence on the right, past a lake on the left, straight over a drive and across a field to the right of a church at the far end, with the pub opposite. Retrace your steps to this point.)

The lovely moated mansion of Groombridge Place was built in the 17th century on the foundations of a medieval house, and the church was built as a private chapel. The walled gardens were laid out under the guidance of John Evelyn and are open to the public. For opening times, tel. 01892 863999.

② To continue the walk, with your back to the bridge turn right for 20 yards and continue on a footpath to the right of a metal gate. Much of the walk follows the **Tunbridge Wells Circular (High Weald) Walk** or its link paths, so look out for the marker posts. The path runs alongside the fence around the grounds of **Groombridge Place** and continues near a canal with boats that carry visitors. Maintain direction over a footbridge, then along the left edge of a field to a stile in the far corner and straight over a stony track. Continue on a path that bends right between hedges laden with blackberries in late summer, then skirts a water treatment works to reach a lane. Go straight across and along the tarmac track opposite. Where this bends right continue ahead down a field, over a footbridge and into a wood at a metal gate. Go right when the path forks after 5 yards and between wire fences to a stile, then go straight on down the left edge of a field, to the right of trees, to another stile. Take the right fork 10 yards on, to cross a field then continue through trees by a stream and into more trees. Cross a stream by a footbridge, then go under a railway. (1¾ miles)

The Spa Valley Railway has restored the line from Tunbridge Wells West to Groombridge, which closed in 1985, and now runs steam and diesel trains on it. The former line, which continued to Lewes and East Grinstead, opened in the 1860s and at one time handled over 100 trains a day. Tel. 01892 537715 for times.

③ The path bends left and continues as a road past **High Rocks** station

DIESEL TRAIN AT GROOMBRIDGE STATION

IN SPELDHURST

and inn. Where the road bends left go straight on through a gap in a wooden barrier fence to walk through trees, with views of fine rock formations on the right and the railway and later a stream on the left.

At High Rocks, the sandstone outcrops and miniature canyons have been a visitor attraction since Victorian times and earlier. Mesolithic people used the rocks for shelter and their hand-axes, dating from around 4500BC, have been found here, while Iron Age Celts had a fort on the top of the rocks.

At a marker post by a gate into a

Woodland Trust reserve keep straight on, then where the path bends right go ahead over a stile. Take the left fork at the next post; fork right 30 yards on and fork left fork after another 30 yards, to walk alongside the railway. Cross a footbridge and continue on a grassy track behind houses. At the end of a block of garages turn right to an estate road then left to a parade of shops. Go left through an archway between shops (**Ropers Gate**) to reach a main road, then turn left to go under a railway bridge. (1 mile)

④ **Tunbridge Wells** is straight on here, but the walk continues by turning left just past the gate to a garden centre, on a tarmac track leading up into trees. At the top of the slope in the wood keep straight on at a junction of paths and continue across a minor road, past ancient oak trees, and straight over tarmac cross-tracks until a main road is reached opposite the **Spa Hotel**. Cross with care and turn left alongside the road to go past a golf club and the end of **Rusthall Road**. Another 400 yards on, keep on the tarmac path as the main road curves off left, to go diagonally right through the trees and bracken of **Rusthall Common** and reach a road by an information board. (1¼ miles)

⑤ Go straight across to another tarmac path then continue up **Lower Green Road** past the **White Hart** pub until you reach the **Red Lion**. Bend right past it then 50 yards on cross to a narrow lane to the right of house no **117**. Where the tarmac ends keep straight ahead on a track between hedges and past allotments. When the track bends right keep straight ahead on a narrower path under trees and bushes to a stile, then on a slightly right diagonal down a field to enter a wood at a stile. Pass a massive beech tree and 80 yards on go right on a wider track, then after 30 yards take the left fork. The path goes through a wood with birch, sweet chestnut, holly and occasional yew and oak. Cross a stream by a footbridge then continue uphill through trees, then bracken, to

SPELDHURST CHURCH

a stile and on between hedges. On reaching a tarmac drive go left on it to a road, then right to a T-junction by the church at **Speldhurst**. There is a fine pub, the **George & Dragon**, 50 yards to the right, but the walk continues to the left alongside the road. (1½ miles)

Speldhurst church has beautiful stained glass by the Pre-Raphaelites Burne-Jones, Morris and Kempe.

⑥ After 500 yards go left opposite **September Cottage** to a metal gate

25

by a footpath sign and on a path behind gardens to a stile. There are fine views ahead as you continue between fences, under holly bushes and down to a lane. Turn right past lovely old cottages, then 100 yards on turn left on a path by the thatched barn at **Old Bullingstone**. Keep left at the fork after 80 yards to go down into a deep ghyll with many ferns growing in the moist, shady conditions. Cross a stream by a footbridge and continue uphill, then follow the marker posts as the wide path winds through the wood. Keep right at a fork by a post, then the path narrows, with a bracken-covered bank on the right. Leave the wood at a stile by a metal gate and continue along the left edge of a field, which is full of purple knapweed attracting many butterflies in high summer. Go straight across a narrow road, then along the left edge of a field to a stile in the far left corner and along the right edge of the next field to a gap leading to a lane. (1½ miles)

⑦ Turn right, ignore the first footpath on the left after 100 yards and continue for 150 yards to the next, then go left on a path across a field and on through a succession of kissing gates, past a large house, **Ashurst Place**, on the right and straight over its drive. Keep straight ahead across the next field to a stile to the left of a gateway and on between fences and over a cross-path via two stiles. Continue along the

right edge of a field and where the fence on the right ends keep straight ahead to reach a road. Go left for a few yards to a main road and cross with extreme care, then go straight up the opposite bank to a stile and over a field, passing two oak trees. At the far right corner you reach a junction of tracks – go straight on, ignoring tracks to left and right, then after 80 yards take the left fork to go between tall hedges. The path soon narrows to reach a stile by a wooden barrier fence, then you continue along the right edge of a field to a stile to the right of farm buildings and ahead on a concrete track. Where the track ends keep right of a gate and follow the left edge of a field, with good views over the surrounding countryside. After 300 yards, as the field edge bends right, go left at a stile in the trees. As the path goes through a wood you may hear the eerie cries of peacocks. Just past a large sweet chestnut the path bends left to a marker post, then right to go downhill to a road. Turn right alongside it to reach the **Crown Inn** at the delightful little green at **Groombridge**. (2 miles)

⑧ From the pub cross the main road with care to a path to the left of the church.

Groombridge church was built in 1625 as a private chapel to Groombridge Place and as a thanks offering for the safe return of

THE MOATED MANOR HOUSE OF GROOMBRIDGE PLACE

Prince Charles from Spain, in the year he was crowned king.

Continue across a field, with views of lovely **Groombridge Place** ahead. Then go over a drive and keep straight on with a lake to the right. The path bends right in front of the house, alongside a metal fence on the left, and continues to the right of the manor and moat. At the end of the house, if returning to the car park at **Groombridge**, turn right over a bridge. Where the track bends right, keep straight on to a path that leads to a gate, then along the right edge of a field to the car park. (½ mile)

If continuing the walk keep straight on at the end of the manor house to the footpath by the metal gate (point 2).

Date walk completed:

KEMSING, KNATTS VALLEY AND HEAVERHAM

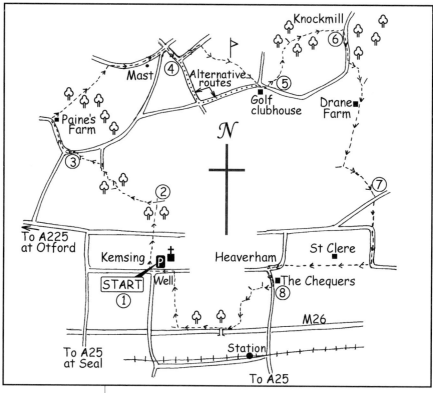

Distance:
9 miles

Map: OS Explorer 147 Sevenoaks & Tonbridge

Starting Point:
The public car
park in Kemsing,
GR 555587.

How to get there: *Kemsing is reached on minor roads
going north from the A25 between Sevenoaks and
Borough Green or east from the A225 at Otford. The car
park is in the High Street, near the Wheatsheaf pub. The
walk could also be joined from Kemsing railway station,
¾ mile from the route (see map).*

THE CHEQUERS INN AT HEAVERHAM IS A LOVELY GEORGIAN BUILDING

*T*he greater part of this circuit takes place on the North Downs above the village of Kemsing. You climb up the steep slope of the downs on springy turf, which in summer is rich in orchids and other colourful flowers, with fragrant thyme and marjoram providing nectar for clouds of butterflies. When you reach the top of the hill there are tremendous views over the surrounding countryside. The walk continues through bluebell woods and along quiet lanes, with the option of an adventurous crossing of a golf course! After descending from the downs, you pass the fine 17th century mansion of St Clere and can indulge yourself in an excellent pub in the hamlet of Heaverham. The route then takes you through farmland and back to Kemsing, where there are more inns as well as a Norman church and an ancient well.

The Chequers Inn in the hamlet of **Heaverham**, towards the end of the walk, is a lovely Georgian building with beams and inglenook fireplaces and a pleasant restaurant in a converted barn. There is also a large garden for summer refreshment. Several Portuguese specialities are available, such as chargrilled chicken piri piri and grilled sardines or mackerel, as well as poacher's pie, containing venison, pheasant, rabbit and wild boar, and rack of lamb with a frangelico jus. The bar meals include tapas, lasagne, salads, jacket potatoes, sandwiches and baguettes. Shepherd Neame ales are served, among them Spitfire and Master Brew.

Telephone: *01732 761413.*

The Walk

① From the entrance to the car park turn right past two pubs and a pleasant area around an old well, then go right on a tarmac path signed to the **Heritage Centre**.

The well in Kemsing is at a spring named after St Edith, the daughter of the Saxon king Edgar the Peaceful. She was born in the village in AD 961 and died when she was 24.

Go uphill past a school and youth hostel/heritage centre to a road. Cross to go up steps to a gate and steeply uphill over downland, which in summer is full of colourful wild flowers such as harebells, eyebright, centaury and fragrant herbs like thyme and marjoram that attract common

and chalkhill blue butterflies. The climb is rewarded by glorious views over the vale below. Keep left of the welcoming benches at the top of the hill to a kissing gate with marker arrows and straight on beneath trees to a cross-track. (½ mile)

② Turn left to follow the **North Downs Way** (**NDW**) long-distance footpath for the next part of the walk, at first between trees and downland, with more fine views. Continue between tall hedges, with more flowers on the banks in season, keeping to the main **NDW** path. At the next open area overlooking a village, go sharp right on the **NDW** at a marker post rather hidden in trees, by a bench. Go up into trees and ahead up steps, then continue with a wood on the left, full of bluebells in spring. At a tarmac drive by a thatched cottage, turn left for 30 yards to a T-junction, then right for

100 yards, before going left on a footpath opposite a house. Keep to the left edge of a field that will be full of chirruping grasshoppers if you are there at the right time of year. Then go through a succession of gates and along the edge of a wood to a road. (¾ mile)

③ Go left, then right along **Row Dow Lane** at a fork. Just past attractive **Paine's Farm**, turn right over a stile, go ahead to another and then straight on across a field alongside the remains of a fence to a stile into trees. Continue on a wide path under tall beeches to emerge at a field, flower-rich in summer, and

go straight on up a slope and into trees to a stile.

Keep straight ahead across a field, keeping just right of a fence around a garden, to a stile by a gate and onto a road. Turn right up the narrow lane between tall hedges and past a telephone mast to a T-junction. Turn left for 50 yards to a crossroads, where there are views to the **Thames**, then go right along **Goodbury Road**. (1½ miles)

④ There is a choice of route here – to avoid a tricky and slightly hazardous route across a golf course, continue along **Goodbury Road**, past **Hills Lane**, and take the next road on

VIEW FROM THE DOWNS ABOVE KEMSING

the left to reach the golf clubhouse, then follow the instructions from point 5. To reduce road walking turn left up **Hills Lane**, then after 300 yards turn right at a footpath sign hidden in trees next to a metal gate. Go up steps to the golf course and keep to the left edge, alongside a wood. Then where the trees end go straight across a fairway with caution and slightly diagonally left past a small pond to a marker post and warning bell. Continue to the left of a green, watching for balls from the left, and follow a gravel track through trees, keeping straight on when it bends left to go downhill, with trees on the left. Proceed on a track through a gap in a fence and steeply downhill to a road. Turn left past the golf clubhouse, passing a road going off left. (¾ mile)

⑤ Opposite the clubhouse car park, go left at a footpath sign behind trees onto a track, and where it bends left keep ahead to the left of a green and right of a pond. Then carefully cross a fairway to a marker post at the edge of trees. Go up through trees and follow the path as it winds through scrub and under trees on the edge of the golf course.

Continue through a wood to a T-junction with a wider path and turn right, soon passing the large trunk of an ancient beech. Follow the path through the wood, full of bluebells in spring, and ahead on a track between houses at **Knockmill Farm** to reach a road. (1 mile)

⑥ Turn right for 400 yards, then left at a footpath sign, to go through the gate of **Whitegate Cottage**. Go left of a tennis court and bend right behind it to a stile in a fence. Continue on the left edge of a field alongside a wood to a marker post, then go slightly diagonally right, away from the wood, to cross a field to the far corner. Turn right through a gap in the hedgeline and go ahead alongside tall beeches, then cross a field to a marker post to the left of a converted stone oast-house. Keep ahead on a dirt track and follow it as it bends left, soon lined by trees.

At a cross-track turn left along the top edge of a field, now back on the **North Downs Way**. Soon after passing a milestone, go left to a stile in a hedge and into trees, then continue along the right edge of a field to enter a wood at a gate. Follow the main path through the wood to a road. (1½ miles)

⑦ Turn right for 30 yards, then left at a footpath sign, to go down steps to a stile, down a steep slope to another, and then straight across a field to a road. Keep ahead along the road for ½ mile, then as it bends left go right on a track past a house. The narrow tarmac road goes past **St Clere** mansion and continues to a road. Keep straight ahead to a T-junction and turn left to the **Chequers Inn** at **Heaverham**. (1½ miles)

St Clere is a mansion of the Stuart period, built in 1631–2 during the reign of Charles I.

⑧ Continue along the road from the pub for 30 yards. Then turn right at a fingerpost to walk alongside a hedge on the right; at its corner go slightly diagonally left across a field to a marker post at the left end of a hedge. Turn left here to cross a small field, then go diagonally right along its right edge. The path curves left at the end of the field, with views to the downs, and then goes through a gap in a wide hedge.

Continue along the right edge of a field; then 20 yards before the end fence turn right at a stile in the hedge and cross a field to the left edge of trees ahead. Keep straight on between the trees and the M26, passing a footbridge over it, to continue parallel to the motorway and cross a footbridge over a ditch. Then go slightly left to a stile at the left corner of a wood. Keep ahead between the trees and the motorway, then along the left edge of a large field.

About halfway along the field edge, turn right past a pond and broken oak tree, aiming for the left edge of a row of cupressus trees, to a stile in a fence. Continue straight across a field to a kissing gate to the left of a house and ahead on a path to reach **Kemsing** village, passing an unusual house with a clock. Turn left along the main street to return to the car park. (1½ miles)

Date walk completed:

33

IGHTHAM MOTE, UNDERRIVER AND THE GREENSAND RIDGE

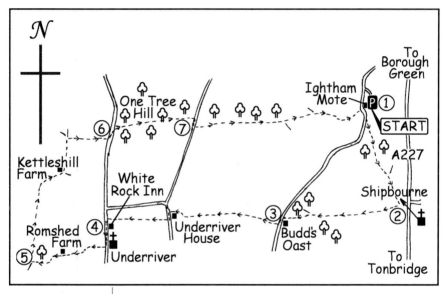

Distance:
7½ miles

Map: OS Explorer 147 Sevenoaks & Tonbridge

Starting Point:
The National Trust
car park at
Ightham Mote, GR

How to get there: *Ightham Mote is signposted from the A227 south of Borough Green and from the A25 east of Sevenoaks.*

THE WHITE ROCK INN ENJOYS A TRANQUIL SETTING

*F*rom the start at the National Trust car park at Ightham Mote, the walk takes you past the lovely 14th century moated house and through pleasant countryside and farmland, interspersed with woods that are carpeted with bluebells in spring. You pass the mansion of Underriver House and can pause awhile at an excellent inn in Underriver village before the gradual climb up a hedge-lined track to the top of the Greensand Ridge. There are wonderful views over the Weald as you follow the ridge over One Tree Hill and through more woods full of wild flowers back to Ightham Mote, where there is a tearoom.

The White Rock Inn at **Underriver**, getting on for halfway round the walk, is an attractive pub in a tranquil setting and with a pleasant garden at the rear. Food can be eaten in the comfortable bars or in the separate restaurant, and the varied menu includes chargrilled steaks, roast duck in a black cherry and cherry brandy sauce, breast of chicken stuffed with Stilton wrapped in Parma ham, and a selection of fish dishes, including lemon sole, monkfish fillet, sea bass and skate wing. There are also delicious desserts such as stem ginger creme brulée, and lighter meals and filled rolls. Ales served include Harveys, Boddingtons, Elgood's Cambridge and Fuller's London Pride.

Telephone: *01732 833112.*

The Walk

① From the car park walk past the ticket office, to the left of the restaurant, and through the staff car park. Follow the road as it bends right, past the lovely old house and moat.

Surely one of the loveliest houses in England, Ightham Mote has a great hall, chapel and crypt dating from 1340, plus a Tudor chapel with painted ceiling and hand-painted Chinese wallpaper. In recent years the National Trust has undertaken an extensive restoration programme. For opening hours telephone 01732 810378.

On reaching a T-junction with a minor road, turn left for 150 yards; then go left over a stile by a gate and along the right edge of a field to another stile. Continue along the left side of a small field to a stile into a wood and follow the path, which can be very muddy at times, through it. From the wood go straight down a field to a large oak tree; then turn left alongside a cupressus hedge. Where the hedge ends, keep straight on for 100 yards and cross a track to a stile ahead. Go diagonally right, keeping right of a copse of trees, and continue with a wire fence on your left to go over two stiles in quick succession and along the left edge of a field to reach the churchyard at **Shipbourne**. (1 mile)

② If you require a pub already, there is a good one behind the church, but otherwise turn sharp right at the edge of the churchyard to take the right-hand of two paths, with a hedge on your right. Continue through a gap in a hedge and straight on across a field to a stile by a yellow pole at the corner of a wood, with a fine view back to the church. Enter the wood on a wide, bare earth track that runs near its right edge. At the crest of a rise, just past where another track joins from the left, take the left fork in the track to keep on the earth track through the remainder of the wood, with gorse and other flowers alongside in season. Keep left at the next fork and continue to a lane. (1 mile)

③ Turn left past **Budd's Oast**, but after 50 yards go right across a green and on a footpath to the right of the entrance to a large house. Continue past its garden and a pond to a stile by a gate, then go straight across a field, through a gap in a hedge, and straight on over another field to a footbridge. Cross two stiles, then go along the right edge of a field to another. You then pass farm buildings and come to a stile. Continue through a metal gate, then walk along the right edge of a field to a stile by a gate. Go diagonally right behind the garden of a large house to a marker post, then left between a conifer hedge and a track road to reach a lane. Turn left and after 150 yards, opposite the impressive **Underriver House**, go right over a stile and straight across a field to a stile by a gate. Follow a line of posts across the next field, then continue ahead over a succession of fields and stiles, and finally alongside tall poplars on the left edge of a field, to

reach a road. Turn left into the village of **Underriver** and the **White Rock Inn** is soon reached on the left. (1½ miles)

④ On leaving the pub, turn left to the church, then just past it go right at a footpath sign to walk along the left edge of a recreational field and then through trees and, bending left, to a gate. From here proceed diagonally right across a field to a stile to the right of a gate and a large tree. Continue to another stile, then go slightly diagonally left across a field, aiming to the left of the farm buildings ahead, to reach a stile 30 yards to the left of a metal gate. Go straight across the road that leads to **Romshed Farm**, the source of the organic eggs on sale in the pub, then diagonally left over a field to a stile by a metal gate. There is a short stretch on a grassy track. Then you fork right alongside a fence; the woods beyond are carpeted with bluebells in spring. You soon reach a stile and a T-junction with a track. (¾ mile)

⑤ Turn right on the track and keep straight on where another track joins from the right later. After ½ mile you pass a large pond on the left with a view over it to a large house. Soon after this a road is reached by a house – turn right on it. On reaching **Kettleshill Farm**, follow the track as it goes to the right of it, then, 10 yards after it bends left past the entrance to a house, go sharp left up a path that runs between wooden post and rail fences and at the back of the oasts of the farm. Continue up a sunken track, with ferns thriving in the shady conditions. The path opens out for a while, with a fine view on the right, and then continues uphill as a sunken track between trees, with beech roots making contorted formations on the banks. When the path opens out again, with metal gates on both sides, turn right on a narrow path just before a wood on the right. You are now on the **Greensand Way** long-distance footpath and will be following it back to **Ightham Mote**. The path goes between a wire fence on the right and a bluebell wood on the left, and after ⅓ mile reaches a road. (1½ miles)

⑥ Turn left up the road past **Carters Hill House**, then after 150 yards go right at a footpath sign onto **One Tree Hill**, a National Trust property. Keep straight on to a marker post after 200 yards, then maintain direction on a broader earth track. There are impressive beech trees in the surrounding woods, and the songs of many woodland birds. Cross a small open grassy area, equipped with a seat to admire the magnificent views across the **Weald**, and continue to reach a T-junction with a

VIEW FROM THE GREENSAND RIDGE NEAR ONE TREE HILL

IGHTHAM MOTE

an undulating track through trees, with a steep slope on the right, to reach a minor road opposite a house. (½ mile)

⑦ Turn right on the road, and after 200 yards go left at a footpath sign to continue with fields on the right and woods on the left. You soon enter the NT **Ightham Mote estate** and go past large rocks and luxuriant, jungle-like vegetation on the slope to the left. Keep on the lower path, where another forks off left, and admire the wonderful views on the right. Go down steps to a track and turn left past a cottage and ahead through more trees, heady with the pungent smell of wild garlic and the sweeter scent of bluebells in spring. There are also other woodland flowers in season, such as wood anemones, celandines and yellow archangel. Later the track becomes stony and then swings left by oasts to a road. Turn right for 50 yards to an entrance gate to **Ightham Mote** on the left and retrace your steps to the car park. (1½ miles)

cross-track. Turn right and soon the path bends right, leaves the NT land at a stile, and then passes the huge trunk of a dead tree, a legacy of the 1987 storm. After this the path takes

Date walk completed:

BOROUGH GREEN, DUNK'S GREEN AND THE FAIRLAWNE ESTATE

THE KENTISH RIFLEMAN AT DUNK'S GREEN IS A VERY POPULAR PUB

Distance:
10¼ miles

Map: OS Explorer 147 Sevenoaks & Tonbridge

Starting Point:
The long-stay pay and display car park off Western Road in Borough Green,
GR 607574.

How to get there: *Borough Green is at the junction of the A227 and A25, south of junction 2 of the M20, with the car park off Western Road (A227). The railway station is a few hundred yards from the start.*

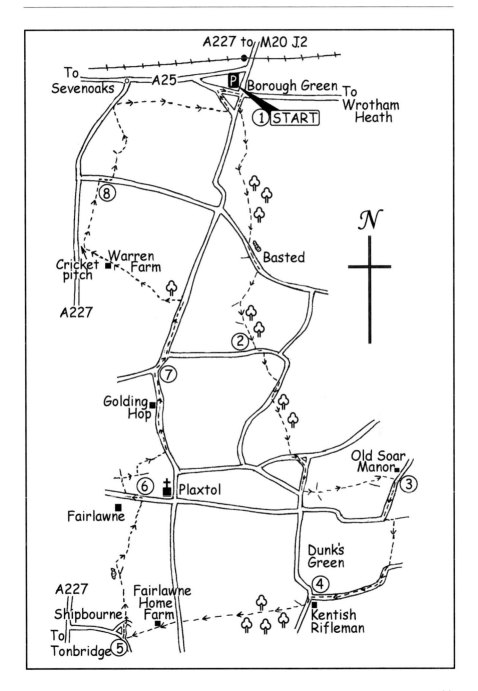

A227 to M20 J2

To Sevenoaks

A25

P

Borough Green

To Wrotham Heath

① START

To Wrotham

⑧

Warren Farm

Cricket pitch

A227

Basted

N

②

⑦

Golding Hop

Old Soar Manor

⑥ ✝ Plaxtol

③

Fairlawne

Dunk's Green

A227

Shipbourne

Fairlawne Home Farm

④

Kentish Rifleman

To Tonbridge

⑤

*T*he countryside south of Borough Green is rarely mentioned in tourist brochures but this walk provides the opportunity to discover how lovely it is. Much of the route goes along the valley of the Bourne, a stream that once powered several mills making fine paper. You pass orchards colourful with pink and white blossom in spring and plantations of cobnuts. There is historical interest in the form of the remains of the 13th century house Old Soar Manor, and the early 18th century mansion at Fairlawne, and many fine views across the valley and to the distant North Downs and High Weald.

The **Kentish Rifleman** at **Dunk's Green**, nearly halfway round the walk, is a lovely old pub, with beams and inglenook fireplaces inside, and a pleasant garden. The extensive range of food offered makes it very popular, examples of the menu being seafood and cream cheese pasta bake, lamb and mushroom pie and goujons of lemon sole. Salads, sandwiches, ploughman's and baguettes are also available, as are Harveys, Fuller's London Pride and Greene King IPA and Abbot ales.

Telephone: *01732 810727.*

 *The Walk*

① Go out of the car park at the pedestrian access at the end opposite the entrance, turn left to a crossroads and cross to the right to go down **Quarry Hill Road**. Opposite the church turn left along **The Landway**, then go straight across an estate road to continue on a footpath behind gardens. The path crosses a drive with a fine avenue of lime trees and then goes through trees and over a stream to a road. Turn left to pass a large pond, formerly a water source for a paper mill, and now home to many ducks. At the end of **Bridge House** on the left, leave the road at the start of **Plough Hill** by going right on a stony track, with a stream on your left. After passing houses the path goes through damp woodland that has a somewhat primeval feel, with its ferns and giant horsetails. Keep to the main path, ignoring a stile on the right, to reach a lane. (1½ miles)

② Turn left for 100 yards, then go right up steps, where a footpath sign is hidden in the hedge, and along the right edge of a field. At a narrow lane by farm buildings turn right for 250 yards, then turn left at a footpath sign just past a small wood to go through trees and then along the left edge of a field. Where the field edge bends left, keep straight on, aiming for the left of the house at the far end of the field, and go left of its garden to a lane. Turn left, then after 100 yards go right along another lane to a T-junction and turn right again. As a road joins from the right, go left on a footpath by a wooden gate. Cross a footbridge over a stream, then keep straight on along the right edge of a field, with tall

alders on the right. At the end of the field keep ahead over a plank and through an area of long grass and weeds. Near the end of the orchard off to your left take the left fork in the path, aiming for the right-hand of two houses ahead. Keep straight ahead up a field to a stile in a fence and hedge around a garden and on past a tennis court to a gate to a lane. (1½ miles)

Old Soar Manor is the remains of a fine 13th century house, once owned by the Culpeper family. The great hall was replaced by an 18th century farmhouse, but the chapel, solar and undercroft remain from

FAIRLAWNE WAS BUILT IN THE EARLY 18TH CENTURY

the original. It is now under the care of the National Trust.

③ It is worth going 50 yards to the left here to view **Old Soar Manor**, but the walk continues to the right along the lane. Where it bends sharp right after ⅓ mile, go over the stile opposite and sharp left alongside the hedge. On reaching a stony track turn right along it and keep straight on where a fork goes off left; where it bends left through a hedge, continue straight ahead to the right of buildings to a lane. Turn right for ½ mile to reach the **Kentish Rifleman** pub at **Dunk's Green**. (1½ miles)

④ From the pub continue in your previous direction for a few yards to a T-junction, then go left along **Dunk's Green Road**. After 100 yards go right at a footpath sign in the hedge, to join the **Greensand Way** long-distance footpath, and along the left edge of a field to a stile. Continue diagonally left across the next field to a stile into a wood, full of bluebells in spring, and from the wood go slightly diagonally left over a field to a road. Cross to the drive of **Fairlawne Home Farm** opposite and continue to the left of the farm buildings and ahead on a stony track to cross a stream, then keep straight on across a field and between gardens to a road. (1 mile)

⑤ Turn right for 50 yards, then right along a narrower lane and soon right again at a T-junction. Where the lane bends right, continue straight ahead on an unmarked footpath to the left of a white house. Go between gardens to a gate and ahead along the right edge of a field, with good views to the **Greensand Ridge** on the left. Where the hedge on the right ends, keep straight on down the field to a footbridge over a stream and ahead to a kissing gate. Keep straight on between trees, then on a tarmac track past an ornamental lake and lovely parkland trees. Pass a wooden seat and 100 yards on turn right opposite the end of a narrow lake to walk alongside a tall laurel hedge and past a massive oak tree. Go up a bank to a stile hidden at the corner of the hedge and a fence. Go ahead to a tall marker post, diagonally left to another, and then maintain direction to a stile in a fence, with views of **Fairlawne** ahead left. Follow a line of marker posts across a field, then go up a bank past trees and walk alongside a fence and past an ornate archway on the left. Where the fence bends left, keep ahead but slightly left to a stile to a road. (1 mile)

The present house at Fairlawne was built in the early 18th century, but an earlier house on the site was the home of the first governor of Massachusetts, Sir Henry Vane, who was beheaded for treason in 1622.

⑥ Walk left along the road with care for 200 yards. Then just past BT premises, turn right over a stile in a metal fence and up the right edge of a field. Your climb is rewarded with a fantastic view back to the **High Weald** in the distance. On reaching a stile in a fence, keep ahead for 10 yards to the end of trees on the left; go diagonally right across a field and past the right end of a belt of trees, and then over a short field and through a gap in trees to an orchard. Turn sharp left and keep alongside the trees on the left to a fence, then turn right between it and a hedge, with views left to the **North Downs**, to reach a lane. Turn left, soon passing some lovely cottages and going down into a shady hollow, with hart's-tongue ferns on the banks. Follow the lane past the **Golding Hop** pub and uphill to a T-junction. (1¼ miles)

⑦ Keep right at the junction to maintain your previous direction, and go straight on where a lane soon goes off right, then continue on the lane between orchards for ⅓ mile, later going downhill and under power lines. Turn left at a footpath sign to go over a stile by a house entrance and along the left edge of its garden,

then the edge of a wood. As the trees end go straight ahead for 80 yards to a tarmac track and diagonally right on it, keeping straight on where another track goes off right. Pass a large farmhouse on the left, then the ruins of a walled garden, and keep left alongside trees where the track forks. At a cricket field on the left go through a gap in the fence and maintain direction along its right edge, past the pavilion and then back onto the track through another gap in the fence. Continue on the left edge of orchards to a lane. (1½ miles)

⑧ Turn right for 150 yards, then left on a path between fences to a cross-path and turn right. The path soon bends left between fields to reach a track by a garden. Turn right, with the garden fence on your left; then go alongside a hedge and between fences, over a stream and straight across a road and soon between gardens to an estate road. Turn left for 50 yards, then right along an alleyway and across a road to another alley. At the next road turn left to a main road and right for 100 yards to the car park opposite. (1 mile)

Date walk completed:

COBHAM, LUDDESDOWN AND UPPER BUSH

THE SHIP AT COBHAM

Distance: 8¾ miles	Map: OS Explorer 148 Maidstone and the Medway Towns
Starting Point: The public car park in Cobham, GR 672685	**How to get there:** From the A2(T) between Gravesend and Strood turn south to Cobham and right into The Street, where the car park is on the right behind the school.

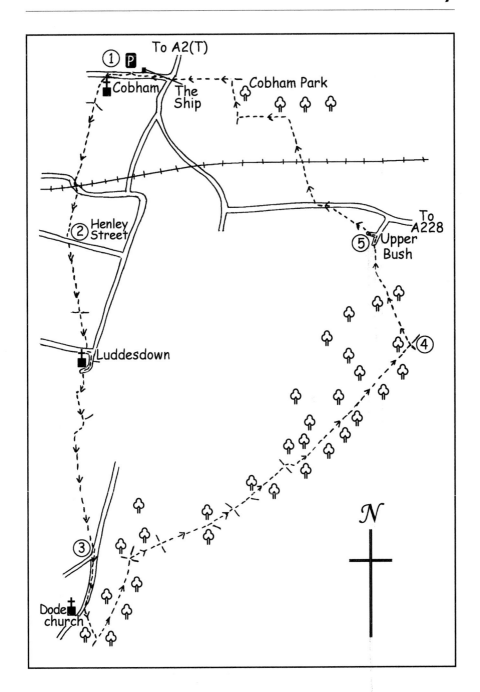

This is a lovely walk through the rolling hills and dry valleys in a part of the chalk downs where Charles Dickens used to roam. It starts at Cobham, with its magnificent church and ancient priests' college, then takes you to a picturesque valley in which the hamlet of Luddesdown nestles. Here there is another ancient church, and you continue along the long scenic valley to the tiny Norman church at Dode. The next section of the walk is through woodland, with displays of wild flowers in spring, before returning through flower-rich meadows and the fringes of historic Cobham Park to Cobham, where there is a choice of inns.

The **Ship**, not far from the car park in **Cobham**, has a good choice of food, including green Thai chicken curry, beef and ale pie, puttanesca pasta and a dish called Hunter's Chicken, with lighter snacks such as sandwiches and jacket potatoes also available. Morland Old Speckled Hen, Greene King IPA, Shepherd Neame Spitfire and Fuller's London Pride ales are served in the comfortable bar areas and there is additional seating outside.

Telephone: *01474 814326.*

 *The Walk*

Cobham church dates from the 13th and 14th centuries and has a unique set of monumental brasses from the 14–16th centuries, considered the best and biggest in England. The almshouses behind the church were built as a priests' college by John de Cobham in 1362.

① Turn right from the car park entrance along the main street. Opposite another good pub, the

Leather Bottle, which has associations with Dickens' *Pickwick Papers*, go left into the churchyard and at the end of the church follow the path round to the left past the historic almshouses and ahead under trees. Continue straight on along the left edge of a graveyard, ignoring a path going off left, to reach a stile. Keep straight ahead down the right edge of a large field, with an orchard and trees on the right, and on through a gap in trees to a lane. Turn left to cross a railway bridge; then, 50 yards on, go right just before a house and along the left edge of a field and through a gap in scrub to a gate. Keep ahead to another gate, then straight on down a field and between gardens to a road. (1 mile)

(2) There is another fine pub, the **Cock** at **Henley Street**, a few hundred yards to the right, but the walk continues by going left for 20 yards to a stile opposite. Go slightly diagonally left up the field to a stile into trees, up steps to another, and slightly diagonally left across a larger field to a marker post and ahead through scrub. As you emerge there is a fine English village scene of cricket pitch and church in the lovely valley below. Continue straight down the field to the right of the pitch and

a former schoolhouse to a lane. Turn left, then immediately fork right on a road to the left of **Luddesdown church**.

The church at Luddesdown dates from the 13th century and next to it is a manor house that originated in Norman times, making it one of the oldest continuously-inhabited houses in the county.

Where the road ends continue ahead through gates on a brick road past houses and bending right, then go left at a stile in the fence, 50 yards on. You are now on the **Wealdway** long-distance path and can follow the

LUDDESDOWN NESTLES IN A PICTURESQUE VALLEY

WW markers for the next part of the walk. Go down a field for 50 yards to another stile, then along the left edge of the next field. Ignore a stile on the left and follow the fence around to the right to go over a stile by a metal gate. Continue along the right edge of fields, on the side of a valley known as **Bowling Alley**, then at a marker post go slightly diagonally left across the corner of the field to another post in the hedgeline. Continue along the left edge of a field, with short grass and downland flowers in season, for 100 yards to a stile in the fence; then go diagonally left down two fields to a stile and up steps to a lane. (1¾ miles)

③ Turn right, then leave the **Wealdway** by taking the left fork after 50 yards. Continue along this narrow lane for 500 yards, and then opposite **Matthewdown House** go left on a track at a byway sign in the hedge. However, before you do it is worth continuing along the lane for 100 yards to view the tiny Norman church at **Dode**, abandoned at the time of the Black Death. The track goes uphill into trees, including some magnificent beeches, to reach a cross-track. Turn left here to follow the **North Downs Way** (**NDW**) long-distance path for the next part of the walk. As the wood opens out on the right, go diagonally right at a marker post, past another wooden post and ahead across a field, under power lines. At the far corner go left through

a gap in a hedge by a metal post, straight across a track, and ahead on a path into trees. Continue straight across a field and over a wide track to a gate into another wood. From the trees go straight over another field and ahead on the main path through a wood. At a wide cross-track follow it to the right, then take the right fork after 30 yards, and a further 80 yards on turn left at a NDW marker on a tree trunk. The path goes through a wood with birch, beech, oak and other trees, with bluebells and other colourful flowers beneath them in spring. Pass under power lines and back into taller trees, with glimpses of the **Medway Valley** through gaps on the right. (3 miles)

④ Where a second set of power lines crosses, with a pylon close on the right, turn left at a marker post and go down a steep slope and steps to a stile out of the trees. Continue down into a valley to the right of a quarry and up into trees, keeping straight ahead to a stile. Go slightly diagonally right across a field to a marker post by trees projecting into the field, then turn right alongside trees on a bank to your left. Follow these trees around to the left; then take a path between tall hedges to reach the hamlet of **Upper Bush**, with a lovely timbered cottage on the left and a view to the M2 bridge over the **River Medway** in the right distance. (¾ mile)

⑤ Leave the **NDW** here by turning left along the narrow lane by the **Upper Bush** sign and where it soon ends continue ahead on a track between farm buildings. Turn right at a marker post at the edge of trees before a gate and go downhill under trees. Continue diagonally left across a field, passing a telegraph pole and keeping right of a hedge that projects into the field from the far end, to reach a lane. Turn left for 200 yards then right at a stile by the gate of **Warren House** (**Abbeyment Kennels**) and along the left edge of the garden for 20 yards to a stile on the left. Continue uphill through a meadow, veering left away from the hedge on the right to reach a crossing over a railway. Cross with great care and then continue diagonally left across a field rich in wild flowers and butterflies in summer, to a stile into trees. Turn left immediately on a track through the edge of the wood and at the end of the trees go right on a wide, stony cross-track to soon reach farm buildings. Go left here along a rough road on the edge of **Cobham Park** to a junction with a road on a bend. Cross with care to **The Street** ahead, with the **Ship** pub soon reached on the right and the car park a short distance beyond it. (2¼ miles)

Cobham Park has a large Elizabethan mansion, Cobham Hall, built in 1584, which has some lovely interiors. It is now a school but is open to visitors on certain dates.

Date walk completed:

TROSLEY COUNTRY PARK, RYARSH AND ADDINGTON

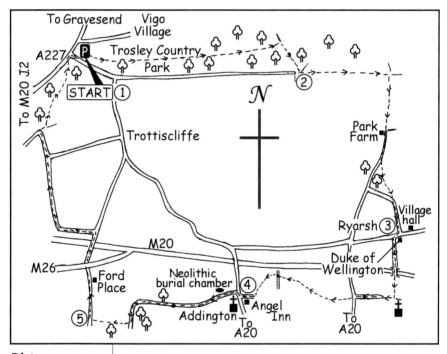

Distance:
8½ miles
Starting Point:
Trosley Country Park car park GR 633611 or alternatively use car park at Ryarsh village hall, GR 671600, and join the walk at point 3.

Map: OS Explorer 148 Maidstone and the Medway Towns

How to get there: *Trosley Country Park is signposted from the A227 north of Wrotham.*

THE ANGEL AT ADDINGTON STANDS BY THE VILLAGE GREEN

Starting through woods of beech and yew on the top of the North Downs, this walk then drops down to the Pilgrim's Way at the base of the hills. After following this ancient route for a while, with many wild flowers alongside in season, you take field paths and lanes to reach the village of Ryarsh and pass its ancient church. You continue over fields to Addington, where there is a fine inn by the attractive village green, and then follow a quiet lane past Neolithic tombs, a bluebell wood and a timbered cottage. The gradual climb back up to the North Downs passes a lovely manor house, then goes between hedgebanks that are flower-strewn in summer. There is a tremendous view as you reach the hills, where a track under overhanging trees leads you back to the start.

The **Angel Inn**, in a lovely setting alongside **Addington** village green – nearly two-thirds of the way round the walk if you are starting from the country park – dates from the 14th century and this history is revealed by the beams and inglenook fireplaces, with log fires in winter. There is a pleasant garden and a non-smoking restaurant with a varied and imaginative menu featuring dishes such as medallions of beef on a potato and garlic rosti, garnished with asparagus in a red wine and thyme sauce. A bar menu is also available offering grilled fish, chicken burritos, omelettes, ploughman's, baguettes and sandwiches, while Courage Best and Directors and John Smith's beers are on tap.

Telephone: *01732 842117.*

 *The Walk*

① From the kiosk and toilets at the car park, go down past an information board to another country park board and a board providing information on the Neolithic megaliths in the area, one of which you will pass later. Turn left at these boards onto a wide track, part of the **North Downs Way** (**NDW**) long-distance footpath, followed for the first part of the walk. Keep on the main track through trees, mainly beech but with patches of dark yews and occasional oak and ash. The track also forms part of the '**red walk**' from the car park – where the track forks after about ¾ mile, keep right, marked '**red walk ext**', then later, where this extension walk goes off left up steps, keep straight on (still **NDW**). The track now bends left uphill to a metal barrier at the boundary of the country park, then 10 yards on turn right on a cross-track to go downhill under overhanging trees to another cross-track near houses. (1½ miles)

② Turn left on a narrower path between hedges, still on the **NDW** but also part of the ancient **Pilgrim's Way** trackway. The path widens out under trees for a while and then becomes narrower again. After ⅔ mile turn right at a marker post on the right, opposite a stile on the left, to go under trees festooned with traveller's joy and with pungent wild garlic beneath, if you are there at the right time of year. Continue over a stile and straight down a field towards a farmhouse, with far-reaching views ahead and left over the **Medway Valley**. At **Park Farm** keep straight ahead along a road for 600 yards; then, where it bends right, turn left over a stile next to a wooden gate and 5 yards on go sharp right on a concrete path along the right edge of a field to a stile. Continue diagonally left across a field to the far left corner and straight on down a lane to reach **Ryarsh** village, with an alternative pub stop. (1¾ miles)

③ Cross to go along **Old School Lane** to the right of the pub, passing houses and an old brickworks, then crossing a footbridge over the M20. Continue ahead on a path between fields to reach a cross-track, with **Ryarsh church** ahead to the left; then turn right and maintain direction as it becomes a road. At a T-junction go straight across to a stile,

ahead to another, then along the left edge of a field to a stile in the far corner. Continue almost straight ahead for 300 yards across the next field; then bear diagonally right to the far right corner. There go down into trees, with bracken beneath, to a stile. Turn left to cross a golf course, watching out for golf balls from either side and aiming between houses and a motorway overhead sign ahead. At a road turn right for 15 yards to a footpath alongside the end house opposite, curving left at the end of the garden to go behind gardens. At a junction with a cross-path turn right; then continue on a lane to reach the **Angel** pub by the

THE LOVELY OLD MANSION OF FORD PLACE, NEAR ADDINGTON

picturesque village green at **Addington**. (1½ miles)

④ From the pub, cross the road to go along **Park Road** opposite, soon passing some large sarsen stones, then flowery meadows with buttercups and the uncommon meadow saxifrage, in season.

The chamber tomb at Addington dates from around 3000 BC. The huge sarsen stones were part of a small chambered barrow, which when excavated was found to contain Neolithic burials. Nearby, the church is mainly of 13th century construction, with a 15th century tower.

Continue on the lane for a mile, past a sports pavilion and village hall, then a disused sand quarry, and through trees with bluebells beneath in spring, later bending left past a lovely half-timbered house and down to a bridge over a stream. Another 100 yards on, turn right at a **Wealdway** (**WW**) footpath sign just past a house to go along the left edge of a field alongside a bluebell wood, where you may see orange tip and peacock butterflies in spring. Continue along the left side of a succession of fields, with superb views to the **North Downs** on the right, and left of gardens to a road. (1½ miles)

⑤ Turn right, soon passing the lovely old **Ford Place**, then two not-so-lovely motorways, going under one and over another, before turning left 150 yards on along **Wrotham Water Road**. This road later bends right between fields and climbs gradually towards the **North Downs** ahead. Keep straight on where a lane joins from the right near a converted oast house, to climb more steeply between hedgebanks. On reaching a T-junction with the **Pilgrim's Way** at the base of the **North Downs**, look back at the fine view and turn right on a stony track. Where the track forks after 100 yards, go left on the **NDW** to ascend the hill under overhanging trees. Later there is a tall brick wall on the right and you continue ahead to the right of a house and through woods full of wood anemones in spring to a main road. Turn right for 50 yards, then right along a lane by the **Vigo** pub. Go downhill for 300 yards; then, just before a footbridge across the road, go left up steps at a **NDW** sign (not along the adjacent bridleway) and left through barriers to return to the car park. (2½ miles)

Date walk completed:

EAST MALLING, THE MEDWAY VALLEY AND BARMING WOODS

THE KING AND QUEEN BECAME AN ALE HOUSE IN 1672

Distance:
10½ miles

Starting Point:
The car park off
East Malling High
St, GR 703569.
Or park at Teston
picnic site,
GR 707534, and
join the walk
at point 6.

Map: OS Explorer 148 Maidstone & the Medway Towns

How to get there: *From the A20 west of Maidstone,
turn off southwards at Larkfield to East Malling. Go
straight on by the King and Queen up the High Street,
with the car park on the left, just before the railway
bridge. The railway station at East Malling is adjacent to
the start and Wateringbury station is also on the route
(see map).*

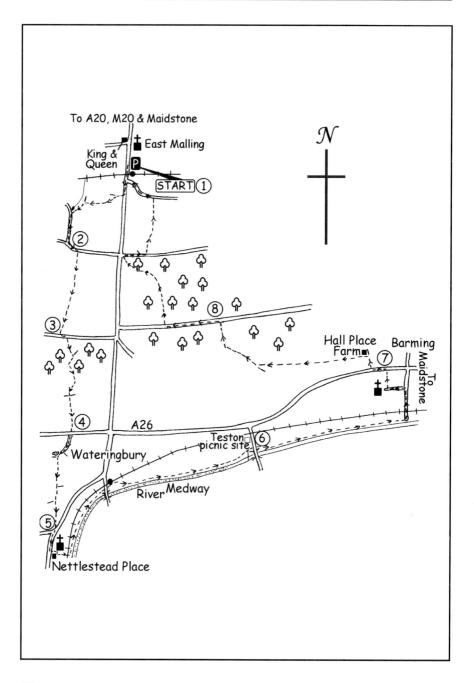

*E*ast Malling is known throughout the world for the work on fruit-growing carried out at the research station there. Starting at the village, which also has a fine Norman church, the walk takes you alongside a spring-fed crystal stream and through sweet chestnut woodland to the lovely church and medieval manor at Nettlestead. There follows an attractive stretch by the River Medway, with the chance to see the plants, birds and insects that live on or near the water. You pass a picturesque medieval bridge, then after more riverside path you climb out of the valley and pass the Norman church at Barming to enjoy more fine views across the valley before returning through woodland and past orchards.

The **King and Queen** has stood near the church in **East Malling** since the early 16th century, when it was built as a dwelling house that was associated with the monastery at West Malling. It became an alehouse in 1672 and probably took its present name when William and Mary were on the throne. It still serves a good range of ales today, from Harveys, Ringwood, Hook Norton and the Flagship brewery at Chatham. There is also a wide choice of food in the large, beamed bar area or separate dining area, with lunch snacks such as baguettes, tortilla wraps, ploughman's, salads, steak and kidney pudding or salmon and broccoli fishcake. Main meals include imaginative fare such as roast red mullet with seaweed and hoi sin sauce and roast duck with caramelised onion and plum sauce.

Telephone: *01732 842752.*

The Walk

(1) From the entrance to the car park turn left under the railway bridge, cross the end of **Rocks Road** and continue ahead up **Chapel Street**. After 300 yards turn right into a passageway alongside **Manningham House** to a kissing gate, then take the left of two paths to go diagonally left across a field to a stile. Keep ahead on a narrow path between a hedge and a fence and at its end turn left to drop down into a delightful valley with a crystal clear stream full of watercress, once grown commercially here. The stream arises from a nearby spring, as evidenced by the names of the lovely old cottages you pass, and once powered

several mills downstream. At a lane turn left to pass, a fine 15th century, timbered hall-house and continue on this lane as it bends left where another road goes off right. (1 mile)

② After 300 yards turn right just past a white bungalow, no **141**, on a path between its garden and trees; then keep straight on alongside tall poplars on the left. The path bends left through the poplars after 400 yards and continues with them on the right. Keep ahead through a gap in a belt of trees; then, where the trees on the right end, go right for 30 yards and then left through a belt of trees. Continue straight across a field, through a gap in a line of poplars, and slightly diagonally right over the next field and through trees to a narrow lane. (¾ mile)

③ Turn left to pass a metal gate across the road and ignore a track going off right just past it, but 20 yards further on turn right at a footpath sign in the trees. The path goes through trees to reach a diagonal cross-track after 50 yards. Turn left to go through sweet chestnut woodland and continue straight on past a huge beech tree in a small clearing; then 40 yards on take the right fork. At the next fork, after 30 yards and near a white concrete post, keep left to continue through woodland for a few hundred

THE CHARMING MILL POND AT WATERINGBURY

yards. As the trees on the right end, there is a fine view over the **Medway Valley**, soon with the white dome of **Mereworth Castle** visible in trees in the distance.

A fabulous mansion built in the Palladian style rather than a castle, Mereworth Castle was built in the 1720s for the Earl of Westmorland. As he didn't want his view from the house spoiled he demolished the nearby village and church and rebuilt them a distance away.

Keep ahead alongside a fence and brambles on the left, ignoring a track forking off right. Where the trees on the left end, keep straight ahead on a grassy path between fences, with orchards on the left, then alongside a security fence around the grounds of a large mansion called Wateringbury Palace, on the right, to reach a main road. (1 mile)

Wateringbury Place was built in Queen Anne style in 1707, using Kentish bricks.

④ Cross with care slightly to the right to go down **Love Lane**, later passing oasts and a former mill to reach a large millpond, home to many ducks. Keep on the tarmac track to the left of the pond and follow it as it bends left, ignoring a footpath going straight on. You pass **Brooms Down** and its walled garden and soon have views along the

valley; then continue past a large converted oast-house and ahead on a path alongside a wire fence, then along the left edge of a field. At its end go through a metal barrier, head right for 5 yards to another; then go on a path between a wooden fence behind gardens and a hedge to reach a main road. (1 mile)

⑤ Go across carefully and turn right alongside the road for 300 yards; then turn left through a lychgate to a path leading to **Nettlestead church**. At its porch turn right for 30 yards, then left alongside a stone wall. Go through a stone archway and head down a field, with the garden of **Nettlestead Place** on the right, to a crossing over a railway and beyond it a path alongside the **River Medway**.

Nettlestead Place is a medieval manor house with an old stone gatehouse and 13th century undercroft. The adjacent St Mary's church has a 15th century nave with some of the original stained glass, though much of it was destroyed by giant hailstones in a storm in 1763.

Turn left beside the river, soon reaching the marina at **Wateringbury**, and continue past the **Riverside Restaurant**, which serves teas in summer, to a road. There is a pub to the left but, if you are not stopping here, go straight across to a stile by a blue gate and ahead on a tarmac track past an old-style

THE SIGNALBOX AT WATERINGBURY

signalbox and a building and down to the riverside by moored boats. As you follow the path alongside the river for the next mile, you may see swans, gulls, terns and possibly a heron or even a kingfisher, while there are patches of colourful flowers such as purple loosestrife and marsh marigold in season. Later the lovely medieval ragstone bridge at **Teston** comes into view and you reach **Teston picnic site**. (2¼ miles)

⑥ Cross the road near the bridge and continue alongside the river, with a view of **Barham Court** to the left. There are footbridges over marshy areas as streams run into the river and dragonflies and damselflies

fly over the vegetation in summer. After a mile you reach a narrow road by a metal footbridge over the river where you turn left under the railway and go uphill past attractive houses. Then turn left along **Church Lane**. About 50 yards before the Norman church at **Barming**, with its elegant spire, turn right at a wooden fingerpost to cross a field to a main road. (1½ miles)

On your right, as you reach the main road, and obscured by overhanging ivy, are the remains of the tiny huts that were the homes for the hop-pickers who, for many years, came from the East End of London to pick the hops in autumn.

⑦ Go across with care and turn left along the verge for 300 yards; then turn right along the drive to **Hall Place Farm**. On reaching farm buildings, turn left through metal gates and between cowsheds, then go ahead on a track along the right edge of a field towards a pylon. Continue past it and alongside a wood, walking parallel to the main road to the left and with a view across the river valley to the early Norman church at **West Farleigh**. Where the trees end keep ahead for 100 yards. Turn right on a cross-track between fields, then with a wood on the right. When you come to a wood in front of you, keep straight ahead on a narrower path into trees to reach a lane. (1 mile)

⑧ Turn left for ½ mile until you reach a hedge on the right, with an orchard behind it. Go right here on a narrow path between the fence and windbreak around the orchard and a wood. Keep straight ahead on this path for ½ mile, going through more sweet chestnut woodland and ignoring any side paths.

The sweet chestnut woods in this area were a source of hop poles, fruit tree support posts and fence posts for many years, managed by coppicing, ie cutting the trees down to ground level on a regular cycle. The tree then produces several fast-growing shoots from the stump.

On reaching some farm huts on the left, keep straight ahead on a narrower path, which bends left at the end of the field on the left. Follow the field edge for 150 yards; then turn right into trees on a track that leads to a lane near a crossroads. Turn right along **Sweets Lane** for 350 yards, then turn left past a wooden gate in a gap in the hedge and follow the main farm track downhill, keeping alongside a tall alder windbreak on the right. You walk between experimental plantations of the horticultural research station and ahead there is a tremendous view to the **North Downs** and along the valley of the **Medway** towards its estuary. Go past a converted oast-house to a road and turn left to go back under the railway and reach the car park or continue past it down the main street to the King & Queen. (2 miles)

The horticultural research station at East Malling is famous for the advancements it has made to fruit growing, including the development of rootstocks that reduce the size of apple, cherry and plum trees, new varieties of raspberry and strawberry, and improved pest and disease control.

Date walk completed:

LINTON, YALDING AND THE GREENSAND RIDGE

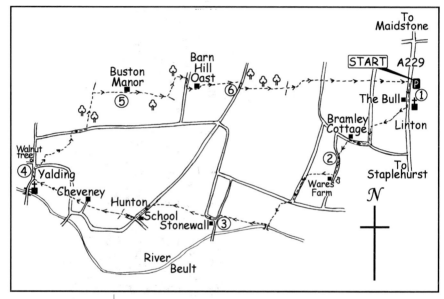

Distance:
8¾ miles

Starting Point:
The public car park at Linton, GR 754503.

Map: OS Explorer 148 Maidstone and the Medway Towns and 136 The Weald

How to get there: Linton is on the A229 south of Maidstone, with the car park on the left at the top of the hill when you are travelling south. Linton is served by buses from Maidstone.

THE WALNUT TREE AT YALDING

*T*his magnificent circuit has wonderful views over the Weald of Kent, with the bonus of blossom-filled orchards in the foreground in spring. The first part of the route descends from the Greensand Ridge at Linton, with views back to its elegant church, and follows the lower ground in the valley of the River Beult. You walk through orchards and fields of strawberries and vegetables in season to Yalding, a lovely village with an impressive medieval ragstone bridge, a 13th century church and many other historic buildings, plus an excellent pub. There follows a gradual climb back up the ridge and then a long section along the crest, past a manor house and alongside woods and orchards, all the while with far-reaching vistas.

The **Walnut Tree** at **Yalding**, halfway round the route, is a very friendly and comfortable pub. The building dates from the 15th century and the bar area still has an inglenook fireplace and original beams decked with locally-grown hops. The bar menu includes beef and ale hot pot with crusty bread and chicken casserole with lemon dumplings, with curries, salads and sandwiches also available. Main meals such as whole sea bass with ginger and spring onions, and lamb shank with honey and rosemary are also served, and there is a separate restaurant. A good selection of ales is on offer, among them Greene King IPA, Adnams, King & Barnes and Fuller's London Pride.

Telephone: 01622 814266.

 *The Walk*

① From the car park cross the busy road with care and turn left past the **Bull**, another good pub – and ideal for refreshment at the end of the walk. A little further on turn right on a footpath alongside the half-timbered **Old Vicarage** to go between gardens and then down the left side of an orchard to a stile by a metal gate. Turn left for 80 yards; then bend right on a track alongside an alder windbreak, looking back for a fine view of **Linton church**, to reach a lane. Go left along it for 300 yards, then right into **Barnes Lane**. After 350 yards go left over a stile opposite **Bramley Cottage** and straight ahead through an orchard; then turn right on a track before a windbreak to a lane. (1 mile)

② Turn left along the lane and opposite the start of a large lake, with cormorants and flocks of geese, turn right over a stile and along the left edge of a field, ignoring a stile on the left to reach another in the far corner. Continue slightly diagonally left across a field to a stile 50 yards to the right of the far left corner. Go left along a lane to a T-junction, then right with care along a road for about 150 yards. Just past a house on the left, go diagonally left through gates on a drive (although not the official right of way, it is used as such while the route is inaccessible). Just before a hedge around a garden turn left on a sandy track alongside the hedge and follow this track through fields, where you may see strawberries growing under plastic tunnels.

The plastic keeps the fruits dry, so reducing the incidence of disease, and they ripen earlier.

66

When you reach a footbridge over the **River Beult**, don't cross it but turn right along the near bank to a footbridge across a stream; then go slightly diagonally right across a large field, keeping 100 yards to the left of the middle of three pylons in the field and aiming for two white-boarded cottages at the far end. Keep ahead between the cottages to a lane and turn left to a T-junction opposite **Stonewall**, a large timbered 17th century house. (1½ miles)

③ Take the road to the right of this house, and just after it bends right by an oast-house cross to a stile and go ahead on a path between hedges.

Continue along the right edge of a field to a footbridge over a stream and walk on the right side of the next field to a stile in a fence. Keep straight on to enter a wood at a stile and from the trees go slightly diagonally right across a field to a road. Cross and turn left alongside the road, then just past a school turn right along **Grove Lane**. Continue straight ahead where the lane becomes a track past fields and when it reaches a farm drive after ½ mile go straight across to a stile and ahead on a grassy track. At a lane turn right for 100 yards then go left on another grassy track and later continue along the right edge of a sports field, past a

VIEW OVER THE ORCHARDS NEAR LINTON

playground and on a path into trees. Continue between hedges and past houses and a churchyard to reach **Yalding** village by a thatched cottage. The church and medieval bridge to the left are worth viewing, but the walk continues to the right, to reach the war memorial, with the **Walnut Tree** pub opposite. (2¼ miles)

The bridge over the River Beult in Yalding was built of ragstone in the 15th century and is the largest in Kent at 100 yards long, with seven arches. The church was also built of ragstone in the 13th century and other fine buildings in the village include the 17th century Court Lodge and Cleaves, where a grammar school was founded in 1663.

④ Go right along **Vicarage Road** by the memorial, now following the **Greensand Way** long-distance footpath back to **Linton**. After 80 yards go diagonally left on a tarmac path and past almshouses to an estate road. Turn left for 100 yards then right into **Mount Avenue** and where it ends continue on a path through trees, later bending left to a lane. Turn right for 250 yards, then turn left at a byway sign just before the lane bends right. (Before you do you may want to look at the orchard on the right, where old apple trees are being preserved.) The muddy track goes uphill under trees and

later with tall poplars on the right. At a gap in them turn right at a marker post to go along the left edge of a field. After 200 yards go diagonally left through scrub, then continue along the right edge of a field, then between fields. Here, and for the remainder of the walk, there are magnificent views over the **Weald**. (1¼ miles)

⑤ Continue on a tarmac track past the partly medieval **Buston Manor** and its 16th century stone barn. Where the track bends sharp left keep straight ahead on an earth track to go past a wood and straight on between fields to a marker post. Here turn left up a field to a marker at the corner of a fence around a wood, then continue ahead to the right of trees for 200 yards to a stile into trees. Go up steps, then turn sharp right on a track and past a gate to a lane. Turn right for 300 yards, then left along a drive to **Barn Hill Oast** and **Jennings Oast**. Where a track to **Jennings Oast** goes off left keep ahead for 30 yards, then straight on to the right of a fence. The path soon bends left and where the fence on the right ends turn right along the left edge of a field, with a bank and trees on the left. Follow a line of marker posts to reach a gate in the fence on the left, then maintain direction, now with the fence on your right. At the end of the orchard go slightly left to a gap in a hedge and take care as you drop down to a lane. (1¼ miles)

THE VIEW TO LINTON CHURCH

⑥ Turn right for 150 yards, then go left up steps and along the left edge of an orchard, with a wood on the left. Just past a marker post keep left of a hedge on a path between it and a wood and continue straight on where a path goes off left into the wood. At a junction with a cross-path turn right for 10 yards, then left on a path between a hedge and a fence. Turn left on a farm track and keep right where it forks to go between an oast-house and converted barn, then ahead on a path alongside a hedge. At a lane cross slightly left to a path between a tall hedge and a fence, keeping straight ahead over a farm track and a cross-path to a stile. Keep straight on along the left edge of a field to a footbridge over a sunken lane and continue ahead across a field, with **Linton church** visible to the right. Continue through scrub and straight across a field to reach the main road opposite the car park. (1½ miles)

Date walk completed:

HARRIETSHAM, THE NORTH DOWNS AND RINGLESTONE

RINGLESTONE INN WAS ORIGINALLY A HOSPICE FOR MONKS

Distance:
9¾ miles

Starting Point:
The car park at
Harrietsham
Community
Centre,
GR 873527.

Map: OS Explorer 148 Maidstone and the Medway Towns

How to get there: *From the A20, turn by the school
into Church Road, signposted to Frinsted and Wormshill,
then turn right into Harrison Drive to the Community
Centre car park. The walk could also be joined from
Harrietsham railway station – a footpath from the coast-
bound platform leads to the avenue of trees mentioned in
point 1.*

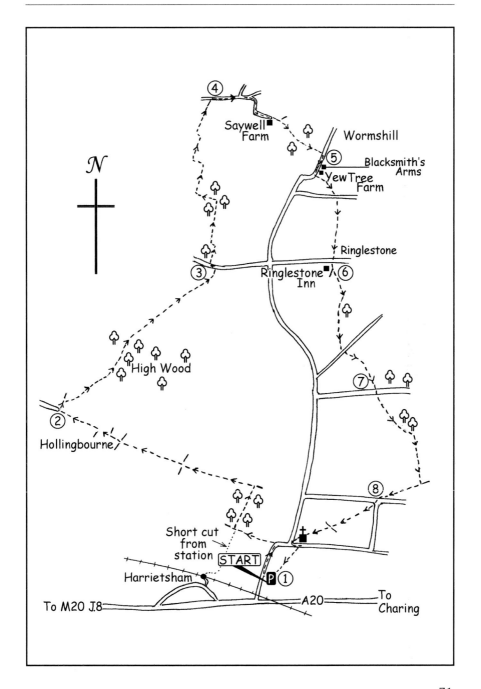

*T*his is quite a strenuous walk, climbing up the North Downs, but it rewards you with tremendous views. Starting in Harrietsham, it follows a long section of the ancient trackway known as the Pilgrim's Way, with cowslips, violets and celandines on the hedgebanks in spring. You then climb up the steep escarpment of the North Downs, with a wonderful view across to the high ground of the Greensand Ridge in the distance. The route continues through woods full of bluebells and other flowers in season and across the gently rolling countryside on the top of the Downs, taking in the hamlets of Wormshill and Ringlestone, which both have good inns. You then descend from the hills through farmland and past the Norman church at Harrietsham.

The **Ringlestone Inn**, about three-quarters of the way round the walk, in **Ringlestone**, was built in 1533 and was originally used as a hospice for monks, becoming an alehouse in 1615. The interior retains the atmosphere of a medieval lamplit tavern, but with modern comforts. You can still appreciate the original brick and flint walls, oak beams and inglenook fireplaces as you quaff your Shepherd Neame or Theakston's ale or sample one of the excellent fruit wines that are available. There is a renowned buffet-style lunch, with a choice of dishes such as cidered chicken casserole, lamb, coconut and banana curry or lamb and Stilton pie. A lovely garden with water features beckons in sunny weather.

Telephone: *01622 859900.*

 *The Walk*

① Turn left from the car park entrance to a road and go right past an impressive private estate with a lake on the left. Where the road bends right, turn left on a tarmac track to pass houses; then go right on a track between an avenue of stately beech trees. Continue to the end of the tree avenue; then go left on a cross-track near a driveway and garden. This is the **Pilgrim's Way** and you follow this ancient track for 2 miles, with wild flowers such as cuckoo pint, celandines and violets on its banks if you are there at the right time of year. Continue straight on over a dirt cross-track after

1¼ miles; then keep left where the track forks to go between bushes, with cowslips and germander speedwell beneath in season. Keep ahead where a path leaves on the left. Then the path opens out, with views of the **North Downs**, and as the track slowly descends there is a far-reaching view over **Hollingbourne** and its manor house. (2½ miles)

② Where the stony track becomes a narrow tarmac road turn right at a footpath sign to go up a track between hedges. Soon after reaching a small wood on the right, enter it via a stile to go through trees with jungle-like lianas, the twisted stems

of traveller's joy, wrapped around them. Climb up steps to a stile; then go diagonally left up a field, with glorious views back to the **Greensand Ridge** as you ascend. At the top of the field turn left alongside the fence for 50 yards, then go right over a stile and slightly diagonally right to soon enter trees. There follows a lovely section along the side of a slope, the woods a blue wash of bluebells in spring under the fresh green beeches and the darker yews. As the path becomes steeper, there are ferns beneath the trees. On exiting the wood go slightly diagonally right across a large field; then turn left on the far side of a

ON THE DOWNS NEAR HARRIETSHAM

fence at the end to reach a lane. (1 mile)

Colourful flowers such as lady's smock, red campion, yellow archangel and celandines appear in the wood in spring, and the songs of birds such as chaffinches, nuthatches and warblers fill the air.

③ Go left for 40 yards, then right at a byway sign on a track along the right edge of a wood and then curving right through trees. After ½ mile leave the wood at a gate, then keep to the left edge of a field. Where the fence on the left ends ignore a stile on the left and keep straight ahead on the track as it crosses a field to a metal gate. Go diagonally left for 20 yards across a wide cross-track to an earthen track between hedges and trees, with wood anemones forming starry carpets in the belt of trees on the left in spring. The track goes down through trees to a minor road. (1¾ miles)

④ Turn right, keeping straight on where another lane leaves on the left; then where the road bends left by barns go right on a road signposted to **Saywell Farm**. Where the track to the farm bends right go straight on through a metal gate and over two stiles. Continue through scrub, then along the right edge of a field to a marker post and down steps to a stile. The path winds down a bank

through trees to a stile in a wire fence, then ahead for 50 yards to another. Go diagonally right across a field to a stile 50 yards to the left of the far right corner and diagonally right up a bank, strewn with primroses in spring, winding your way through trees to a stile. Keep straight ahead over a field to a stile in a fence between the gardens of the two right-hand houses of a row and ahead to a road. (1 mile)

⑤ Turn right through **Wormshill**, with an alternative pub stop, the **Blacksmith's Arms**, on the left. Continue past **Yew Tree Farm**, then as the road bends right, turn left over a stile and cross the field on a slightly left diagonal and go down to a marker post on the edge of trees jutting out into the field on the left. Continue through a wide gap in a tall hedge and diagonally right across the next field to the far right corner and over stiles to a lane. Go straight across to a stile and ahead along the left edge of a field to another; then cross the next field to a stile at the edge of a wood. Continue around the left edge of the wood to a stile; then go straight ahead down a trackway and through a gate to soon reach a minor road, with the **Ringlestone Inn** to the right. (1 mile)

⑥ The walk continues to the left of the pub when facing it, over a stile opposite the **Farmhouse Hotel**. Go diagonally left across the field, keeping just right of the telegraph pole in the middle, to a stile in a gap in the hedge. Continue across another field, aiming for the left edge of a wood ahead, to go over a stile and turn right alongside a fence and through scrub to a marker post. Turn left across the grassy area of a caravan park to a stile by an old rusty tractor, then go on a slightly left diagonal across a field to a lane. Go straight across to a stile, through scrub and alongside a hedge on the right to another stile, then ahead across a field past two large trees and a wet area by trees to a stile by a metal gate and onto a road. (1 mile)

⑦ Cross to a stile; then go diagonally left across a large field to a stile and ahead between wire fences to another. Keep ahead to the first telegraph pole in the field, then slightly diagonally right on a sunken grassy path down to a stile. Continue slightly diagonally left down the next field, past a telegraph pole, aiming for the factory ahead, to the left-hand of two stiles in a fence around a horse paddock. The right of way crosses the paddock by going diagonally sharp right over stiles in the paddock fences. From the last stile go straight across a long field, just to the left of the left-hand telegraph pole in the row down the field centre, and aim for the far corner, to the right of houses, to reach a road. (1 mile)

Parts of Harrietsham church date back to Norman times and it contains an unusual font from that period. Its tall tower was built in 1480.

⑧ Cross diagonally right to a stile by the end of **Marley Road** opposite and head diagonally left towards **Harrietsham church** in the distance. Go through a gap in a fence, and 300 yards on cross a stile on the right; then go sharp left for 100 yards to another. Continue straight ahead to a stile by a metal gate, over a cross-path and diagonally right across a field to a kissing gate and ahead on a path that skirts the churchyard and reaches a road. Turn left for 50 yards, then go diagonally right across a grassy area to a kissing gate and head between houses to the car park. (¾ mile)

Date walk completed:

CRANBROOK AND GOUDHURST

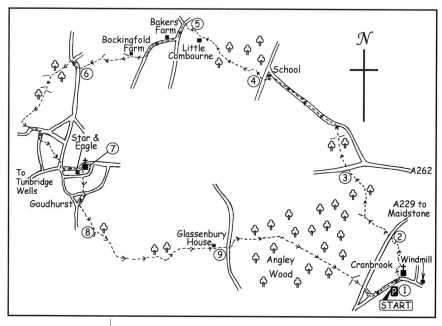

Distance:
10¾ miles

Starting Point:
The public car park in Cranbrook, GR 774359.

Map: OS Explorer 136 The Weald

How to get there: *Cranbrook is just off the A229, with the car park on the south side of the High Street.*

THE STAR AND EAGLE AT GOUDHURST CAN BE TRACED BACK TO THE 14TH CENTURY

*T*he starting point for this walk on the Kentish Weald is the attractive small town of Cranbrook, which rose to wealthy prominence during the 14th century with the introduction of the wool weaving trade from Flanders. This wealth is reflected in the magnificence of the church and several large houses from the period. The largest and finest smock windmill in the country, built in 1814, stands proud above the town. The route takes you through bluebell woods and pleasant farmland, with fantastic views as you approach Goudhurst, a lovely village with a large duckpond and some fine buildings, including a wonderful church. It also has two good inns and a teashop to provide refreshment. You return to Cranbrook, where there are several hostelries and cafés, through farmland and woods.

Once home to a notorious gang of smugglers, the **Star and Eagle** inn at **Goudhurst**, more than halfway round the walk, can trace its history back to the 14th century. It has a scenic exterior of timbers and a balcony, while inside the beams and inglenook fireplaces also indicate its age. The spacious bar areas offer beers such as Boddingtons and Adnams, and there is some fine food on offer there and in the restaurant. Examples include *moules et frites*, roast shoulder of lamb Spanish style and chicken fajitas, plus daily specials and a delicious dessert menu. Bar snacks such as filled baguettes are also available. At the rear of the inn is a patio with terrific views over the Weald.

Telephone: *01580 211512.*

 *The Walk*

Cranbrook contains some fine houses, many dating from the 14th to 16th centuries, when it was home to people who had become rich from the wool weaving trade. The white weatherboarding in the town is typical of many places in the Weald.

① Go out of the car park entrance and turn right along the **High Street**. Where the road bends right, take a path near the **tourist information office** that leads left into the churchyard. Keep left of the impressive sandstone church to the far end of the churchyard and ahead on a road to the left of a recreation ground, then on a path between hedges to a kissing gate. After 20 yards go right on a footpath that soon bends left between school playing fields. After another gate go diagonally left across a field to a kissing gate by a wooden barrier at the edge of trees and on a narrow path to a main road. (¾ mile)

② Go straight across with care to a track, soon past a rugby field. About 200 yards past a bend, leave the track at a kissing gate on the left to continue parallel to it through trees. Soon there are paddocks to the left and a bluebell wood on the right. Where the paddocks end turn right at a marker post to go along the right edge of a wood. Continue straight on at the next marker post to go through a wood and later cross a stream. The path becomes a stony track between large houses and ends at a main road. (1 mile)

③ Cross with care to a footpath sign opposite and go onto a path between gardens and through a wood. At the end of a chainlink fence on the right, go over a cross-track (ignoring arrows pointing left and right) to a stile behind a holly bush. Cross a track and another stile and go across a field to a stile in the far corner, then down a bank to a lane. Turn left along it, the banks colourful with bluebells, stitchwort and wood anemones in spring, until after ½ mile you reach a school sign. Here go left on a path that goes behind the school and bends right to a road. (¾ mile)

④ Go straight across and along the right edge of a field to a marker post by a tree, then on a path between a wire fence and a hedge. Enter a wood at a stile and keep straight on at a stony cross-track, to continue between conifers and birch. From the wood go straight over a field into another smaller wood, with celandines and other flowers in season. Continue along the right edge of a field, then right of a pear orchard and on a concrete track past a house. The track becomes stony, with primroses on the banks in spring and fine views ahead, then bends right by **Little Combourne Oast** to reach a minor road. (1 ¼ miles)

⑤ Go left for 10 yards to a T-junction, then left along the lane. Where it forks keep right into **Ladham Road**, soon passing the lovely half-timbered **Bakers Farmhouse** and a converted oast. After the lane bends left down a hill, ignore a footpath going off right on a track and continue uphill for 300

THE REWARDING VIEW NEAR GOUDHURST

yards; then turn right on a tarmac drive to **Bockingfold Farm**. Pass a cherry orchard on the left and take the left fork in the drive by a farmhouse to keep left of a large oast-house; then curve gradually right alongside its garden. Keep straight on at a marker post where a concrete drive goes off right, to continue ahead on an earth track along the right edge of a field. Continue downhill across another field, over a stream and ahead on the left of a poplar hedge. At a T-junction with a cross-track in front of a hedge, keep left on a grassy path alongside a tall hedge on the right, soon passing a lovely black and white house to reach a busy road. (1¼ miles)

⑥ Cross with extreme care on the corner and turn right on the verge opposite. After 200 yards, as the road bends right, go left on a footpath just past a house and down a sunken path between trees. Keep straight on through a wood, with a pond on the right, to a stile, then diagonally left to the left-hand of two footbridges ahead. Continue along the left side of a field for 300 yards to a marker post, then left through bushes to a stile, then keep to the right edge of a field alongside a wood, where you may see early purple orchids in May. From the next stile, cross a field to a track between wire fences that continues to the left of a converted oast-house ahead and bends left as a drive to reach a lane

on a corner. Keep straight ahead; then turn right at a junction with another lane. After 150 yards go over a stile on the left and on the left edge of an old orchard, with giant horsetails in the damp areas. Continue up the left edge of a field, with a wood on the left, to a stile, then diagonally right up a steep incline to a stile in the far right corner of a field. There is another steep climb up the next field to a stile in the far left corner, but the reward is the glorious views back over the verdant countryside of the **Kentish Weald**. A narrow path leads from the stile, between houses, to the village of **Goudhurst**. Turn right to a T-junction near one good pub, the **Vine**, and the picturesque duckpond, then left to reach a tearoom and the **Star and Eagle** inn. (1½ miles)

⑦ From the **Star and Eagle** go into the adjacent churchyard and before the church entrance turn right down a path with a handrail to a road. The route back to **Cranbrook** follows that of the **High Weald Landscape Trail**, a long-distance path, so look out for the markers. Cross to the footpath opposite and go downhill between fields, then down steps to another minor road. Turn left for 20 yards, then take the right fork and, just before this road reaches a junction, turn left down a track next to a house. On reaching a metal gate on the right, go over a stile into a field. Keep to the left edge, skirting a riding paddock, and at the field's end cross a stile to a road in front of new houses. Go down a path next to the left end house. (¾ mile)

⑧ At the end of the garden on the right, go left on a grassy path that leaves the main track and goes along the left edge of a field alongside a wood. From the next marker post go over a footbridge, straight on to the next post and over a track. Continue near the left edge of a long field with rough grass and rushes to the next marker, then go left on a track. Soon leave the track to go right of trees and a large pond and continue parallel to it, keeping straight on where the trees end to follow the left edge of a field to the next marker. Follow a farm track past another pond to a stile by a gate, then slightly left to another after 100 yards. Proceed along the left edge of a field to a stile. Turn right on an earth track and follow it as it bends sharp left, with fine views back to **Goudhurst**, perched on the distant ridge. The track bends right and passes a house. As it bends past the house, go straight on at a marker post and along the left edge of a field with the garden of the large **Glassenbury House** on the left. Cross a footbridge at the end of the field and continue along the left edge of a large field to reach a road. (1¾ miles)

⑨ Go straight across to a gate, then diagonally left around the left edge of a field to reach a track. Turn right on it to soon go into trees between tall banks and into bluebell woods. Just past a woodcutters' corrugated iron hut, leave the track as it bends left to go straight on at a marker post, over a stile and through conifer and birch trees, with heather beneath. Keep straight on at the next post, on a wider track, then, at a wide diagonal cross-track, go diagonally left on it. Continue straight ahead, ignoring any cross-tracks and crossing a deeply-cut stream at one point. Where the track bends left, go straight on at a marker post (not diagonally right) to wind up through trees on a narrow path. On reaching a deep cleft, turn right on the near bank and keep alongside it to a post. Turn right for 10 yards, then left on a narrow path and left again at a cross-path. At a broad track turn right and follow it through the rest of the wood to a main road. Cross with care and go straight ahead on a road between houses. At the next junction turn left along the main street through **Cranbrook** to reach the car park. (2 miles)

Date walk completed:

TENTERDEN AND ROLVENDEN

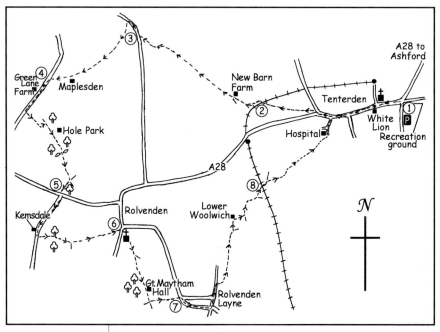

Distance:
10¾ miles

Map: OS Explorer 125 Romney Marsh

Starting Point:
The public car park in Recreation Ground Road, GR 886334.

How to get there: *From the A28 running through Tenterden, turn south at the eastern end of the town alongside the recreation ground into Recreation Ground Road. There are regular buses to Tenterden from Ashford, Maidstone and Tunbridge Wells.*

THE WHITE LION IS A 16TH CENTURY COACHING INN

*G*oing through lovely rolling countryside on the high ground above Romney Marsh, this walk provides the opportunity to step back in time with a view of a steam train on the restored Kent & East Sussex Railway. Tenterden is a lovely town, sometimes known as 'the jewel of the Weald', and has a wide, tree-lined main street and several historic buildings, including a church that can be seen for miles around. The route also passes some grand houses, among them Great Maytham Hall and Hole Park, and goes through the pretty village of Rolvenden, with its white weatherboarded cottages and 12th century church.

There is a wide choice of pubs, restaurants and tearooms in **Tenterden**. The **White Lion** is a 16th century coaching inn and provides a good selection of ales, including Adnams Broadside and the Reverend James from Brains, in pleasant surroundings with beams, inglenook fireplaces, old photographs and other memorabilia. There are salads, jacket potatoes and sandwiches with imaginative fillings such as Portobello steak with onion chutney or goat's cheese, basil and chargrilled vegetables, making a meal in themselves. Light meals include gammon ham with bubble and squeak cakes, poached eggs and hollandaise, and pan-fried liver and bacon with garlic mash and brandy cream sauce and there is a full restaurant menu.

Telephone: *01580 765077.*

The Walk

① From the car park walk up to the main street and turn left. Pass the **White Lion** on the left, opposite the church, cross the road and continue for ½ mile, past a road going off left to **Rye** near another pub. Continue alongside the road past a hospital entrance opposite, then turn right into **Cranbrook Road**. After 30 yards turn left on a footpath at a metal gate and go slightly diagonally right across a field, past a large oak tree to a stile in a fence, then diagonally right over another field to a stile in the far corner. Keep straight on for 20 yards; then turn right through a metal gate to cross a railway. (1¼ miles)

The Kent & East Sussex Railway closed in the 1950s but has been restored by enthusiasts and now runs steam trains from Tenterden to Bodiam Castle. Tel. 01580 765155 for details.

② Continue ahead to cross a footbridge, then go sharp left, parallel to the railway, to a stile 30 yards to its right and hidden in the hedge. Cross a footbridge and stile and walk ahead to a gateway in a hedge; then maintain direction across the next field, aiming left of farm buildings ahead, and look back for a view to **Tenterden church**.

The church tower at Tenterden, built of Bethersden marble in the 15th century, is 120 feet high and is visible for miles around.

Continue through another gateway, then left of a telegraph pole and farm buildings, to a stony track opposite a house. Turn right to go between farm buildings, left of a white house; then go through a wooden gate and along the left edge of a field. Continue ahead on a track between hedges and later a concrete track. Just before the impressive **Halden Place**, go right through a gateway on a concrete track and straight on where it ends, to cross a field to a stile in the far left corner and reach a lane. (1¼ miles)

③ Turn right, passing **Mount Pleasant Farm** with its pond and oasts, then, just before another oast on the left, turn left over a stile at a wooden fingerpost and along the right edge of a field to another stile. Continue on the left side of a field alongside trees to a marker post and straight ahead to the left of a clump

of trees around a sunken area to another post at the end of a line of trees projecting out into the field. Proceed on a slightly right diagonal across the next field to a stile by a metal gate, 100 yards before the far right corner. Turn sharp left on the field edge for 200 yards to cross a footbridge in trees on the left, then go straight ahead between hedges. The path becomes a wider track under trees, with pleasant views of rolling countryside. At a newly-planted orchard keep straight on to a gate, through an open barn, and ahead on a concrete road past a large house and oasts to a lane. (1¼ miles)

THE TREE-LINED MAIN STREET IN TENTERDEN

④ Turn left to pass **Green Lane Farmhouse** and, having ignored the first fingerpost on the left, go left at another, 500 yards on, and over a stile next to a gate saying 'TAPA Private'. Go along the left edge of a field to a stile by a gateway, then left alongside a hedge with a walled garden and greenhouses beyond, to a stile by a wooden gate. Turn sharp right here on a narrow path between hedges and on emerging from trees maintain direction on a gravel drive, with **Hole Park** mansion to your left. At a T-junction with another drive go straight across to a stile in a metal fence, behind a horse chestnut tree. Continue diagonally left across a large field, keeping left of the first clump of trees, then right of two large trees, and finally right of a large horse chestnut, and go through long grass by conifers to a stile (marked path **AT40**). Keep straight on between two ornamental lakes to a stile in a fence, then ahead to the left of a pond and trees. Go slightly left as you proceed up the field, aiming for a windmill that comes into view, to reach a narrow tarmac road and turn right to a main road. (1½ miles)

⑤ Cross with care to go along the lane opposite for almost ½ mile, then left up steps at a fingerpost to a kissing gate. You are now on the **High Weald Landscape Trail** (**HWLT**) and can follow the waymarkers back to **Tenterden**. Go diagonally left across the field to the left corner of a wood, then ahead to

a stile into it, immediately over a plank bridge and up through trees, to leave the wood at a stile. Continue along the right edge of a field to a stile and ahead to a metal gate, ignoring another on the right. Go diagonally left over a long field to a stile in the far left corner, 100 yards to the right of a corrugated barn. Keep straight across a smaller field to a stile in a hedge, slightly diagonally left over a meadow. Then turn left alongside trees and, shortly before houses, bend right through the trees to go along the left edge of a school playing field to a road opposite a church. (1¼ miles)

⑥ The **Star** pub at **Rolvenden** is to the left but the walk continues straight across to the right of the church and through the graveyard, keeping straight on where the brick path forks to a kissing gate. Continue diagonally left down a field, with fine views ahead, to another gate, then diagonally right, through a gap in the hedge and ahead, to the left of tall sycamores, to a gate into a wood. Keep straight ahead on a track and straight on where it bends right to continue on a narrower path between fences, with rhododendrons flowering in season and the grounds of **Great Maytham Hall** on the left.

The grounds of Great Maytham Hall contain a walled garden which inspired Frances Hodgson Burnett to write 'The Secret Garden'.

After a dark section beneath conifers, cross a stile, then go sharp left for 20 yards to another and along the left edge of a field, then on a path between fences to a stile by a pond. Turn sharp right along the right side of a field and through two gates to a road. (1 mile)

⑦ Turn right along **Maytham Road** to go through the village of **Rolvenden Layne**, with the option of visiting the **Ewe and Lamb** pub or **Woodentops** tearooms. At the crossroads by the tearooms, turn left, and continue straight on along the lane where another joins from the left. Just past **Upper and Lower Winser Cottages**, go right at a **HWLT** fingerpost along a gravel drive to a gateway to a house, then diagonally left past a metal gate. Continue straight across a field, through a gap in a hedge and turn sharp left on the field edge, following it as it bends right for 20 yards. Then go left down steps at a marker post. Go through trees and straight over the next field to a post by a fence. Turn sharp right for 100 yards to cross a stile, then maintain direction for 20 yards to a farm track and keep ahead on it to another marker post. Turn left up the field and follow the **HWLT** markers to go right past a house, then downhill alongside a hedge. Go left up the bank at a marker post in the hedge and straight across a field; then go ahead to the left of a marshy area with rushes and across a meadow to a post by a large willow tree. Cross a footbridge and keep ahead to a post, then straight on (not left) along the left edge of a field alongside a ditch. Cross a stream by a marker post and go along the left side of a field to another post, sometimes accompanied by the croaking of marsh frogs in the ditch. Cross a bridge over a wider dyke; then go slightly diagonally left to a stile by metal gates. (2 miles)

⑧ Cross back over the railway, then go diagonally left for 50 yards in front of tall alders to a footbridge, then sharp right for 100 yards to another. Keep ahead for 50 yards to a hedge and maintain direction alongside it, along the left edge of a long field to a stile in the far left corner. Continue along the right edge of the next field to a stile in the hedge and straight over a field towards buildings in the trees. Turn right at a post for 100 yards, then left through trees, parallel to a hospital drive. At a T-junction with a narrow road, turn left on it to a main road. Cross with extreme care to the pavement opposite and turn right to retrace your steps along **Tenterden High Street** to the car park. (1½ miles)

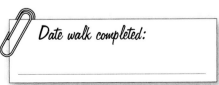

Date walk completed:

WYE, THE STOUR VALLEY AND BOUGHTON LEES

THE FLYING HORSE AT BOUGHTON LEES OVERLOOKS THE GREEN

Distance:
10¾ miles (plus extra 1 mile extension to and from pub)

Starting Point:
The public car park at Wye, GR 053468.

Map: OS Explorer 137 Ashford

How to get there: *Wye is reached by minor roads running east from the A28 to the north of Ashford. Cross the bridge over the river and turn left into Churchfield Way; the car park is on the right opposite the green. The route passes Wye railway station (see map).*

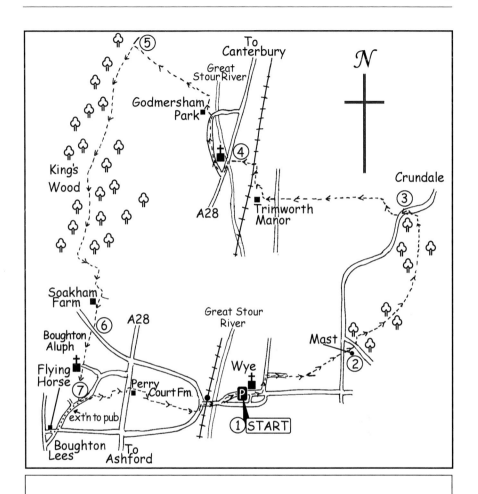

*T*his walk takes you through some of the loveliest countryside in Kent. It starts at Wye and from there you climb up the Downs, with wonderful views over the Stour Valley. You then drop down to pass the lovely little church by the river at Godmersham. The walk continues through parkland and climbs back up the other side of the valley. There follows a section through woodland, with displays of bluebells in spring, then you pass the ancient church at Boughton Aluph and have an optional diversion to a good pub at Boughton Lees and you return to Wye through orchards, with another good pub alongside the river there.

The **Flying Horse** is on the green at **Boughton Lees**, towards the end of the walk, and is an old pub with beams, stone-arched windows and a big inglenook fireplace. The pleasant bar area serves meals such as breaded scampi or plaice, and chicken and bacon salad, and offers a good choice of beers, including Greene King IPA, John Smith's, Courage Best and Shepherd Neame Spitfire. There is a separate restaurant and among the dishes available you could find breast of chicken with tarragon and mushroom sauce and rack of lamb with garlic mash and redcurrant jus. A spacious garden, rose-filled in summer, also makes a pleasant place to sit in good weather.

Telephone: *01233 620914.*

 *The Walk*

① Turn right from the car park entrance to go past the church and the oldest of the college buildings, founded in the 15th century, then turn left into **Olantigh Road**. Just before the large Kempe building, turn right along **Occupation Road** to go past glasshouses and other university buildings. Where the road and buildings end, keep ahead on a track for 500 yards. Then go diagonally left at a marker post to cross a field towards a phone mast and over a stile in trees, then right to a lane. You are following the long-distance **Stour Valley Way** for this part of the walk. Cross the lane to a stile; then follow a tarmac track to the mast and continue on a path to the left of it, going through trees and over a cross-track to a sunken lane. (1 mile)

② Go straight across and up steps, then through trees to a field. Turn sharp right along the field edge, then as it curves right, go diagonally left at a marker post to climb the field to a stile in trees in the far corner, with a wonderful view along the **Stour Valley**. Continue uphill through trees to another stile and straight ahead across a field that is being managed for restoration of its downland flowers. From the stile at its end keep ahead to another on the right of a metal gate. Then 80 yards on go right near a large ash tree to head towards a gateway but turn left in front of it on a path between a hedge and wire fence. Go along the right edge of a wood, then, where the field on the right ends, keep straight ahead through trees, now with a wire fence on the left. Continue on a grassy track through the wood and downhill into a valley. As you emerge from the trees, with views ahead, go sharp left, then curve right, keeping to the upper edge of the field. This field edge is a naturalist's paradise of colourful chalkland flowers in season, including bee, fragrant and pyramidal orchids, scabious, eyebright, thyme, marjoram and knapweed, and these attract common blue, brown argus and meadow brown butterflies. At the end of the field go straight on into trees in the far left corner but soon go left on a wide earth track, then right at a marker post after 40 yards and through trees to a lane. (1¼ miles)

③ Leave the **Stour Valley Walk** here by going left past a large house, then just after a left bend go right over a stile in the fence and up a field to a ridge, from which there are fantastic views. The path from here is not clear but the route goes diagonally right, along and down from the ridge, to a stile to the right of a metal gate in the far corner of the field. Continue downhill on a grassy path between fields, then ahead on a farm track to the left of a hedge. At a road go straight across and along the drive to **Trimworth Manor**, then where it forks turn right over a stile and along the left edge of a field to a stile by a house. Go straight across its drive and diagonally left across a field to a railway line. Then continue to the right on a path between fences

THE WIDE OPEN SPACE ABOVE THE STOUR VALLEY

alongside the railway and after 400 yards turn left through an archway beneath it. Continue on a raised bank towards a church and reach a main road. (1½ miles)

④ Cross with extreme care and go left on a footbridge over the **River Stour**, then after 100 yards turn right up a minor road. You pass the lovely flint church at **Godmersham**, well worth a look, and then bend right on the lane past a long barn and alongside the wall bordering **Godmersham Park**. Where the road bends right go through the second set of metal gates on the left, then immediately right through a pedestrian gate and on a path alongside a metal fence. Keep straight on for 300 yards when the fence ends, passing lovely parkland trees, then go left at a marker post on a path between fences and newly-planted hedges, with fine views of **Godmersham House** on the left. Keep straight on over a cross-track near **Deer Lodge**. Then the stony track climbs uphill to a stile by a gate, with lovely views back over the mansion and valley. Continue on the track for 100 yards; then go slightly diagonally right to a post and follow a line of posts up the field to a stile in a fence, with a view to **Canterbury Cathedral** through a gap to the right. Maintain direction across another field to a post and stile in trees. (1½ miles)

Godmersham Park is a lovely Georgian mansion, built in 1732. Jane Austen was a frequent visitor here in the late 18th and early 19th centuries, when her brother owned the estate.

⑤ Turn left on a track, part of the **North Downs Way** long-distance path, which is now followed back to Wye, first through the edge of **King's Wood** for 1¼ miles. Many of the mature beeches were lost in the 1987 storm but you will still see some fine specimens, plus lots of sweet chestnut and some larch, and there are carpets of bluebells in spring. In season, speckled wood butterflies bask on leaves or engage in aerial dogfights over territory. Keep left at a fork at the end of the first clearing on the right to stay alongside the fence at the edge of the wood for a time, then the path gradually veers into the wood. Where a track joins from the left, bear right at a marker post then keep straight on at a cross-track after 200 yards. At a point 50 yards before a stile at the end of the wood, turn left on a cross-track at a marker post and continue near the right edge of a wood, with fields beyond. Where the path divides, take the branch that goes sharp left and soon goes downhill, later with views to the right and ahead across the valley to the crown carved in the hills above **Wye**. Continue through a metal gate and swing right between banks, then bend left and right to a farmyard and

ahead on a track to a road.
(2½ miles)

King's Wood was once a royal hunting forest and you may catch sight of the fallow deer that still roam here. Look out for hoofprints in soft ground.

(6) Cross with care on the blind corner and go ahead on a path that soon bends left and right between hedges, ignoring a stile on the right. Continue straight ahead across a field towards a church, over a stile between gateways and across a field to a stile and road. Go straight over, to the left of the ancient church at **Boughton Aluph**, and along a narrow field to a kissing gate, then go ahead alongside a hedge and under overhanging bushes to a lane. (1 mile)

(7) The walk continues to the left here but should you wish to visit the pub at **Boughton Lees** turn right, keep left where a lane leaves on the right, and continue to a T-junction, with the village green and pub ahead to the right, then retrace your steps

to point 7 (½ mile each way). Follow the lane to a left bend; then go right through a metal kissing gate and sharp left to follow the left field edge past farm buildings and alongside a hedge. At the end of the hedge turn sharp left for 250 yards alongside a fence, then at its corner go right across a field to a main road. Cross and turn left past the entrance to **Perry Court Farm**, which has a good farm shop, then after 30 yards turn right over a stile in the hedge and go along the left edge of an orchard. Go through a gap in a windbreak and ahead on a farm track, keeping left as other tracks fork off right. At a marker post go right for 50 yards and then left on a track alongside a tall windbreak, with **Wye church** visible ahead. Keep straight on across two fields and a meadow to a road; then left for 200 yards to a T-junction. Turn right past the railway station, go over the **River Stour**, and reach another excellent pub, the **Tickled Trout**, then bear left along **Churchfield Way** to return to the car park. (2 miles, not including pub extension)

Date walk completed:

CHILHAM AND PERRY WOOD

THE ROSE AND CROWN STANDS AT THE EDGE OF PERRY WOOD

Distance:
7¾ miles

Starting Point:
The car park at
Chilham,
GR 067537.
Alternatively park
at Perry Wood,
GR 045556, and
join the walk at
point 3.

Map: OS Explorer 149 Sittingbourne & Faversham

How to get there: *Chilham is at the intersection of the
A28 and A252, west of Canterbury, with the public car
park signposted from the A252. Chilham railway station is
½ mile from the start (see map).*

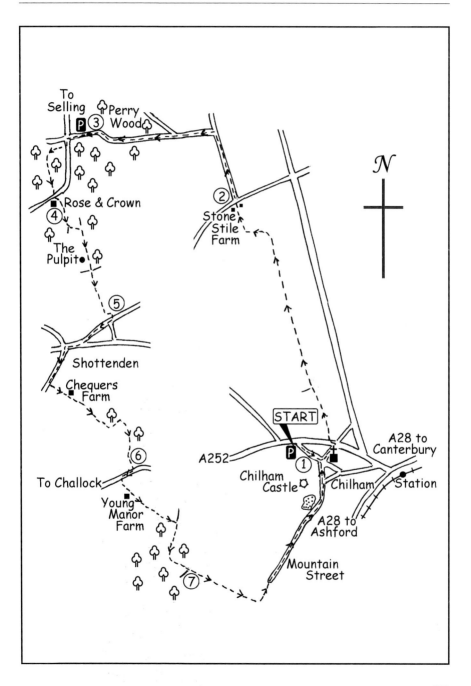

*T*his circuit starts in Chilham, one of the loveliest villages in Kent, with its wealth of medieval timbered cottages and hall-houses. There is also a beautiful 15th century church and a large Jacobean mansion with a 12th century castle keep. A pub and tearoom are available if you require refreshment at the start or end of the walk. The route goes past orchards that are colourful with blossom in spring, through woodland and past the site of an Iron Age fort to high ground with wonderful views for miles around. There is a welcoming pub on the edge of the wood, then you return to Chilham through woods that are carpeted with bluebells in April and early May.

The **Rose and Crown** is a friendly pub in a lovely setting on the edge of **Perry Wood**, reached when you have completed just over a third of the walk. It dates from the 16th century and has beams and inglenook fireplaces with roaring log fires in winter, while for warmer conditions there is a large garden, colourful with flowers. The choice of ales includes Harveys, Goacher's and Adnams and there is a good selection of food, ranging from sandwiches, ploughman's and jacket potatoes to full meals. These include pies such as chicken, ham and leek or rosemary lamb, and crispy Chinese chilli beef, while examples of specials are salmon and prawn crumble and Moroccan lamb with couscous. You will also be tempted by some delicious desserts.

Telephone: *01227 752214.*

The Walk

Chilham has many houses dating from the 14th to 16th centuries, making attractive groupings in and around the square. The Jacobean mansion known as Chilham Castle

was built in 1616, but has a 12th century keep.

① From the car park entrance turn right to the main square. Keep ahead to the **White Horse** pub, an alternative for refreshment at the end of the walk, and go down **Church Hill** to the left of it. After passing delightful cottages, you reach a main road. Turn left for 50 yards and cross with care to an unmarked path to the right of a tall hedge, near a telegraph pole. Go through a gate, and then continue to the left of a line of tall poplars, with orchards to your left. Where the poplars end keep straight on under power lines, to the left of an alder windbreak. Keep ahead over a tarmac farm track and straight on where the windbreak on your right ends, now with one on the left. At its end keep straight ahead through a gap in a windbreak that crosses your path and go gradually uphill. Keep to the right side of a windbreak and ahead through a gap in another where the former ends. After 100

yards the track bends left to a T-junction with a tarmac track – turn right to reach a road by farm buildings. (1½ miles)

② Cross to go along the lane opposite and follow it past white-painted cottages, then turn left on another lane. Keep straight on where a road goes off right opposite **Three Beeches** and continue on the lane through a wood for ½ mile to a car park on the right. (1 mile)

③ Continue past the entrance (turn right from it if starting from there) for a few yards to a crossroads. Turn left for 30 yards; then turn right past a gate at a bridleway sign. After a short

THE NORTH DOWNS NEAR CHILHAM

THE VIEW FROM PERRY WOOD

distance take the right-hand track at another sign and follow it as it curves left along the top of a bank, with the earthworks of an ancient fort on the left. Keep left of picnic tables and go downhill on a shingle path, to emerge from the trees opposite the **Rose and Crown** pub. (½ mile)

Perry Wood forms the highest point in this part of Kent and offers superb panoramas of the surrounding countryside. There was a fort here in prehistoric times and flint tools have been found.

④ The walk continues on a bridleway to the left of the pub and its car park. Keep right of a gate

leading to a house, and after skirting its garden go left at a fork in the path by a short marker post. The shingle path goes uphill through bracken, with wonderful views behind as you climb higher. At a T-junction with a cross-path, turn right and keep on the main path, with more far-reaching views on both sides. After passing a clump of conifers you reach a raised viewing platform known as '**The Pulpit**'. The path continues to the left of the platform and picnic tables and descends a slope via steps. At the bottom of the slope keep ahead over a cross-path to a stile. Go along the right edge of an orchard, alongside a windbreak; then swing left behind a garden and turn right where it ends

to reach a stile onto a road. (¾ mile)

⑤ Turn right past houses to a T-junction; then go right for 200 yards to a crossroads and take the left turn towards **Deane Manor**. Pass a small chapel converted into a house, and on reaching power lines turn left on a tarmac track at a byway sign. Where the tarmac ends at **Chequers Farm** continue on a dirt track between hedges, with the flowers of knapweeds and scabious attracting gatekeeper and meadow brown butterflies in high summer. Follow this track for a mile between hedges and fields, alongside a wood, then curving left through trees and continuing to a main road. (1½ miles)

⑥ Cross with care and turn right on the verge for 100 yards; then go left on the drive to **Young Manor Farm**. As it bends right keep straight on over a stile, then diagonally right across a field to a fence and a line of trees and follow them uphill to a stile

at the left edge of a wood. Keep ahead over a farm track and along the edge of the wood, with a fine view along the valley to the left. The path goes into trees and soon reaches a broad cross-track at a marker post. Turn right through the bluebell wood, keeping on the main track and ignoring one going off right. Pass a huge, ancient beech tree and keep left at a fork near a dead tree to bend left through conifers. (1 mile)

⑦ Where the **North Downs Way** footpath joins at a gate on the right, keep straight on, soon with good views on the right over **Godmersham Park** and the **Stour Valley**. The path bends left and reaches a road. Keep ahead along it, later passing some fine timbered houses at **Mountain Street** and the lake of **Chilham Castle**. On reaching **Chilham** village, go straight ahead up **School Street** to the main square and then left to the car park. (1¾ miles)

Date walk completed:

BEKESBOURNE, ICKHAM AND LITTLEBOURNE

THE DUKE WILLIAM AT ICKHAM DATES FROM 1611

Distance: 8½ miles	Map: OS Explorer 150 Canterbury & the Isle of Thanet
Starting Point: The car park at Bekesbourne railway station, GR 190560.	**How to get there:** *From the A2 just east of Canterbury, take the turn to Bekesbourne and turn left into Station Road. Then, go left along Station Approach to the car park, which is adjacent to Bekesbourne railway station on the line from Canterbury East to Dover.*

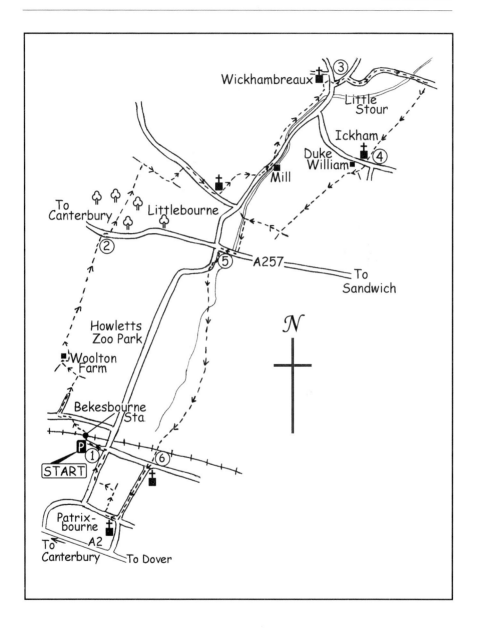

A route that takes you through several lovely villages, each with a pub to delay you. If you manage to complete the circuit despite these temptations, you will see picturesque watermills alongside rivers and streams, impressive tithe barns, timbered houses and thatched cottages. There are also ancient churches with wonderful stained glass and a fantastic carved stone archway, dating from Norman times. The pleasant countryside through which you walk has many streams and orchards, with remnants of sweet chestnut woodland.

The **Duke William** pub at **Ickham**, just over halfway round the walk, has a larger interior than the external appearance suggests. The building dates from 1611, but there is a lovely modern conservatory at the rear which also has the advantage of being non-smoking. You can choose to eat there or in the bar area or restaurant, your appetite whetted by a menu that includes smoked trout, breast of chicken butterfried with fresh ginger on a bed of onions, or specials such as monkfish with a Chablis cream. There are also omelettes, jacket potatoes and baguettes, while ales such as Adnams, Charles Wells Bombardier and Shepherd Neame Master Brew are served.

Telephone: *01227 721308.*

The Walk

① From the station car park cross the footbridge over the railway to the opposite platform, then go left on a path running parallel to the platform and accessed by a gate. Go straight across a track to an alley that leads past the **Unicorn** pub to a minor road. Turn left for 200 yards before going right along a narrow lane, just past the entrance to farm buildings.

After passing houses, keep straight on where the track ends, along a path with trees on the right. On reaching a field, keep to the right edge alongside a windbreak hedge, and where this ends go left on a wide track between fields, which had plastic tunnels over strawberries when I did the walk. At the cross-track at the end of the field go straight across into trees for 20 yards to a stile, then ahead across a small field. Turn right on a gravel drive, then left after 30 yards, between farm buildings, towards an old thatched barn and diagonally left on a tarmac drive in front of it. Take the right fork after 100 yards to swing right alongside a windbreak. At a large barn the right of way takes the right fork, to go past cottages, and then curves back to rejoin the tarmac drive, on which you continue until a main road is reached. (1½ miles)

② Cross with care to a hidden gateway and footpath sign in trees, 50 yards to the right, and go past a white gate and ahead on a track through trees, mainly sweet chestnut. A Roman road used to run through this wood, but there is no sign of it today. Where the wood ends, continue straight on between hedges

until you reach a stony cross-track near a phone mast. Turn right on the track and follow it, passing a cottage and later curving left to reach a road. Go right along the road until you come to **Littlebourne church**, then left through the lychgate and through churchyard, noticing the impressive thatched tithe barn alongside.

Littlebourne church dates from the 13th century and contains an old wall painting of St Christopher.

Keep right of the church to a gate in the far corner of the churchyard and a stile 5 yards on. Continue ahead across a field to a stile, then on a

NEAR LITTLEBOURNE

path that skirts a garden to reach a road. Turn left, then, opposite the lovely white-boarded watermill, go diagonally left on a stony track for 5 yards, then ahead on a path running parallel to it. Keep to the right edge of fields, soon with the **Little Stour river** alongside and views of a tall watermill and the 14th century church at **Wickhambreaux** ahead.

Littlebourne watermill has white weatherboard cladding on a brick lower storey and was built in the late 17th or early 18th century. Milling continued until 1943.

At the field's end bend left to the churchyard and go through it via a gap in the wall to reach the village green, which is surrounded by fine manor houses and cottages. (2¼ miles)

Surrounding the green at Wickhambreaux are the attractive Wickham Court, with its green shutters and Doric porch, and the early 18th century Old Rectory, plus a gabled cottage of similar date. The 14th century church has a spectactular Art Nouveau window of 1896 by Baron Rosenkrantz.

③ Head across the green and go down **Gutter Street** to the right of the **Rose** inn, then turn right opposite the thatched **Tudor Cottage**. Follow this lane for ⅓ mile, bending right to cross the river again, with the arch of a former watermill

A WATERMILL ON LITTLE STOUR RIVER NEAR LITTLEBOURNE

visible at **Seaton Mill**. A little further on, turn right just past a white house onto a concrete drive and keep straight on where it ends to go between fields towards **Ickham church**. Keep left of the churchyard to a road, with the **Duke William** pub to the right. (¾ mile)

④ The walk continues from opposite the church, on a bridleway next to **Dove Cottage** and past a large converted oast-house. Continue on a slightly right diagonal across a field to a marker post, then left on a stony track. Where the track ends near a house, turn right at a marker post to cross two fields to another post, then ahead past a garden and over a footbridge to a track. Turn left to walk alongside a river and reach a main road, then go right alongside it to another good pub, the **King William IV** in the centre of **Littlebourne**. (1 mile)

(5) Cross the road with care near the pub and go straight ahead across the green, with a row of attractive cottages on the left. Where the green ends maintain direction along **Bekesbourne Lane**, then where it bends right go left along a drive to **Garrington Farm**. The drive goes through marshy areas and over a stream. Where it bends left by houses keep straight on along a track, which becomes a grassy path past a cottage. Continue through a gate, straight across a stony track, then keep near the left edge of a field, with a bushy bank on the left. To the right is a stream along the valley and beyond it you may glimpse the remains of a chapel and, in the distance, the animal enclosures at **Howletts Zoo**. At the far left corner of the long field, go through a gateway on the left and immediately right through another, then diagonally right across a field towards a wooded railway embankment, under which you pass through a long brick archway.

Continue along the right edge of a field to a road. (1½ miles)

(6) For a short-cut back to the station, saving ¾ mile, turn right along the road to a crossroads and straight across up **Station Approach**. To continue the walk, which passes more

lovely buildings, cross the road to **Old Palace Road**, 10 yards to the right, and go along it, crossing a ford near **Bekesbourne church** and the old palace.

The Old Palace, near the ford and church, is the remains of a huge palace built in the 1540s during the reign of Henry VIII but mostly destroyed during the 1650s. Archbishop Cranmer wrote the book of common prayer here and Ian Fleming, author of the James Bond books, also lived here.

Continue for another ⅓ mile to a T-junction near another ford. It is worth a short diversion to view **Patrixbourne church**, just to the left ahead.

However, the walk continues to the right at the T-junction. Then, 100 yards before a fine black and white timbered house, go right at a gap in the hedge. The path goes past gardens and a recreation ground. Then, 100 yards on, turn left by a solitary poplar tree to cross a field to a road. Turn right alongside it, then left at a crossroads to return to the station car park. (1 mile)

Date walk completed:

RECULVER, MINNIS BAY AND SARRE

THE CROWN INN AT SARRE

Distance:
11¾ miles

Map: OS Explorer 150 Canterbury & the Isle of Thanet

Starting Point:
The car park at
Reculver Country
Park, GR 226693.

How to get there: Reculver Country Park is signposted
from the A299 east of Herne Bay, with the car park
behind the sea wall.

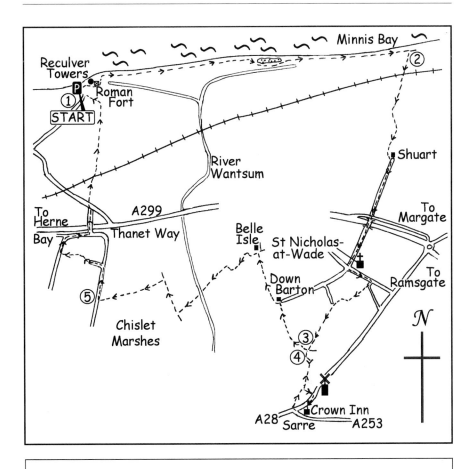

*B*eginning at the atmospheric setting of the twin towers of an ancient church on the edge of the sea at Reculver, this walk passes the remains of a Roman fort there, before going along the sea wall to Minnis Bay. This section offers a wonderful opportunity for some birdwatching, as many waders and gulls congregate on the shoreline. The walk then goes inland to the village of St Nicholas-at-Wade with its impressive church, Dutch-gabled houses and pubs. You continue to Sarre, where you pass a restored windmill with a tearoom on the way to an excellent inn. The return to Reculver is across farmland and reclaimed marshland, before the landmark towers come into view.

The turn off to the **Crown Inn** at **Sarre** is reached just over halfway round the walk. This friendly pub, which dates from the 16th century and has the priest's hole to prove it, offers good food served in pleasant surroundings. The bar menu includes spicy chicken pasta, mussels, and spinach and ricotta cannelloni, while in the restaurant you can feast on lamb shank in red wine sauce, breast of pheasant or duck breast with a kumquat sauce. A range of Shepherd Neame ales are served, or you could treat yourself to the speciality of the house, a cherry brandy made to an old and secret recipe, enjoyed by several celebrities such as Charles Dickens and Douglas Fairbanks, as well as my wife, who hardly noticed the rest of the walk!

Telephone: *01843 847808.*

The Walk

The church at Reculver was built in the 12th and 13th centuries on the site of a 7th century monastery, and the towers date from the late 12th century. Nearby is a fort built by the Romans to defend the Wantsum channel.

① From the car park, take the tarmac track past the towers of the ruined church to a T-junction with a cross-path, and turn left to the sea wall, then to the right along it. Follow the track along the wall for 3 miles, with the opportunity to spot birds such as oystercatchers, turnstones, cormorants and curlews and plants like yellow horned-poppy and sea pea that are adapted to grow on the inhospitable shingle. Go straight on where the track bends in and out past a lagoon at **Coldharbour**, another good spot for birdwatching, as redshank and other waders feed in the shelter of the sea wall. Continue until you reach the edge of **Minnis Bay**, with the buildings of **Birchington** opposite. (3 miles)

② Go right down steps to a footpath fingerpost, signed to **St Nicholas-at-Wade**, and walk inland on a raised track to the right of stables and a barn. Where the track bends right, keep straight ahead to cross a railway line with care and continue along a grassy track through a marshy area and then between hedges. After going to the right of farm buildings, the track reaches a lane. Turn right along the lane for ½ mile to a T-junction, where you go straight across the first road to a footbridge over a main road. Continue ahead along a lane to a T-junction by the church at **St Nicholas-at-Wade** and turn left past attractive cottages and two pubs, should you require refreshment at this stage. Turn right down **Manor Road** by **The Forge** and where it soon bends left go straight on to the right of a black and white cottage, then on a path to the left of a recreation ground. At the far left corner keep straight ahead on a tarmac path that crosses a field and then bends right and left past gardens. Where the gardens end keep straight ahead on a path between large fields to reach a gate at the hedgeline. (2¾ miles)

③ If you do not wish to do the extra loop to the pub at **Sarre** (1 mile there and back), turn right here on the track alongside the hedge. Then follow the instructions from point 4. For **Sarre**, go straight on through the gate and on a path between hedges, then fields. At the corner of a wood, turn left to a main road opposite a smock windmill, built in 1820 and now restored (tearoom available), then cross with care and turn right alongside the road, to soon reach the rear of the **Crown Inn** in **Ostlers Lane** on the left. To return to the walk after the pub stop, go out of the front entrance and turn right to a T-junction. Cross carefully at the end of **Canterbury Road** to a marker post for the **Wantsum Walk**, then go straight ahead for 20 yards to a narrow path to the right of a white house. Continue between hedges, past trees on the right, and on

BUILDING BEGAN AT RECULVER CHURCH IN THE 12TH CENTURY

between fields and hedges to return to the metal gate, where you turn left on the track alongside the hedge to continue the walk. (1 mile)

④ Keep to the left edge of the field, then, where a concrete track joins from the left, keep ahead but slightly left to a marker post, then over a stream and through an area of parked caravans to a metal gate in the far right corner. Turn sharp left here on a path to the left of farm buildings, then between fields with a dyke alongside on the left. On reaching an isolated white house go left along a concrete track and follow it over a dyke, where you may see a heron fishing, and remain on the track as it bends right and left. Where the concrete ends, go straight ahead to cross the narrow **River Wantsum** and continue on a stony track.

At a T-junction with a cross-track in front of a dyke, turn right and keep alongside the dyke, ignoring two narrow footbridges over it. Then turn left on a track that goes across the dyke, past a metal gate. Follow the track between fields, over a cross-track, and continue until a lane is reached. Much of this area was occupied by saltworks in the past. (3 miles)

⑤ Turn right along the lane, past the **Hog and Donkey** pub. Then, just past

Redrow Cottages on the right turn left along **Reynolds Lane**. Where the road ends keep ahead on a path that curves right between hedges, then along the left edge of a field to a gate to a tarmac drive. Turn left along the drive to a road and right to a T-junction. Turn right along the road to go parallel to the main road beyond; then cross it at a road bridge on the left after 400 yards. At the next T-junction cross slightly to the left to a concrete track alongside a house which has the tower of a windmill nearby. The track forms part of the **Saxon Shore Way**, and the towers of **Reculver** are a welcome sight ahead. It goes under a railway, then as it later bends right, follow it for 20 yards, going left at a marker post to cross a dyke and continue along the left edge of a field towards the towers ahead. Cross a footbridge, and continue along the left edge of a field, keeping straight on where the dyke alongside veers away left. On reaching a track by a caravan park, turn left along it to a road, with the car park opposite to the right. If you want further information about the history and wildlife of the area, visit the **Kent Wildlife Trust information centre** at the end of the car park. (2 miles)

Date walk completed:

_____

ELHAM, THE ELHAM VALLEY AND DENTON

THE JACKDAW AT DENTON

Distance:
9¾ miles

Starting Point:
Park in the square near Elham church, GR: 177438.

Map: OS Explorer 138 Dover, Folkestone and Hythe

How to get there: *Elham is on a minor road between Canterbury and Lyminge. From junction 12 of the M20, go west on the A20 and turn off northwards through Lyminge, then turn right in Elham into the square by the church.*

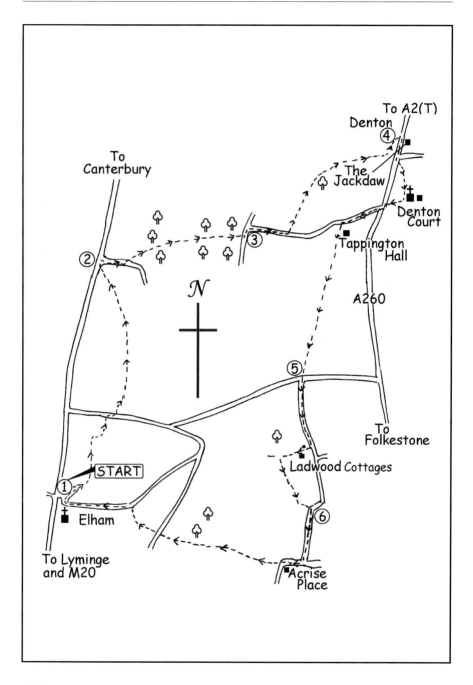

This walk goes through beautiful downland countryside, starting at the village of Elham, in its picturesque valley setting. There are lovely timbered cottages in the village and a fine church, dating from around 1200. The route takes you along the scenic Elham Valley, through grassland full of colourful wild flowers in season, across fields and through small woods to the next valley. Here you drop down to Denton, with its fine pub, manor house and 13th century church. You return through rolling countryside of fields and woods, watched by grazing sheep, and finish with a magnificent view over Elham, where several pubs await you, should you require further refreshment. This is an undulating walk with several tall stiles.

The **Jackdaw** at **Denton**, 4 miles into the walk, was built in 1645 as a farmhouse and later became a coaching inn. It is still popular with travellers today, with a wide range of food and drink served in comfortable surroundings. There is a good choice of ales such as Young's, Tetley's, Castle Eden, Ringwood and Shepherd Neame, while meals include roast duck with a black cherry and Tia Maria sauce, steak and Stilton pie and a luxury fish pie, with specials such as shark supreme wrapped in banana leaf with pineapple rice. There are Sunday roasts, sandwiches, ploughman's and clotted cream teas, with food served in the bar, separate restaurant or garden.

Telephone: *01303 844663.*

 *The Walk*

① From the square go down **Cock Lane** to the right of the **King's Arms**, a good place for refreshment at the end of the walk. The lane ends at a gate. Go diagonally right across a small field, through another gate,

and sharp left along the left edge of a field with poplars and the **Nailbourne** stream on your left. You are now on the **Elham Valley Way** footpath, which on this section follows the route of the former railway along the valley. The path bends left and right to a stile, then along the left edge of a smaller field to a lane. Turn right for 30 yards, then left along a drive to a gate and

113

slightly diagonally right across a field to a stile in a fence, then sharp left to cross another. Keep straight on along the left edge of a field to a marker post and follow the markers for the **Elham Valley Way**, first by going diagonally right, then on through a gap in a hedge and along a grassy valley to the corner of a fence. Continue along the left side of a field, up a bank to a stile in a fence, then straight on alongside a line of telegraph poles and down to a stile in the far left corner of the field. Go down the next field, aiming left of farm buildings ahead, to a stile in the far left corner. (2 miles)

The Elham Valley Railway used to run along the valley from Canterbury to Folkestone. It opened in 1887 and was used for huge rail-mounted guns during World War II, before closing in 1947. Little is visible now, but a bridge can be seen on the opposite side of the road reached at the end of point 1. There is a museum with information about the railway in a former station at Peene, to the south of Elham, on the edge of Folkestone.

② Turn right along the road here, taking care as the verge narrows, then after 100 yards go right along a

THE MAGNIFICENT VIEW OVER ELHAM

lane. About 100 yards past houses on the right and as the lane starts to bend right, go through a gateway on the left, with a marker post hidden in the hedge, and then diagonally right up the field to a stile in trees. Continue through an old hazel coppice to a tall stile, straight ahead across a field to a stile in a hedge, and then slightly diagonally left across the next field. At the far end leave the **Elham Valley Way** by going straight up the bank to a stile, slightly right across a field, then straight across a track and diagonally left to stiles in a double fence.

Maintain direction across the next field to a stile at the edge of trees and go down through them to another stile. Turn left alongside a fence for 80 yards, then right downhill between fences to a metal gate and ahead up a bank to enter a wood at a stile. Keep straight ahead on the main track through the wood and past a garden to a lane. (1 mile)

③ Turn left, then soon right along another lane. Where the hedge on the left ends after 400 yards, go left at a hidden fingerpost and straight across a large field, then continue to the left of large ash trees and later a wood. At a gap in the wood go right for 20 yards to a marker post, then sharp left on a path through trees.

As you leave the trees there are lovely views over the valley and to the 17th century mansion of **Broome Park** in the left distance. Go down

the left edge of a field, then left on a tarmac path past houses and **Denton village hall** to a main road by fine timbered houses and cross with care to the **Jackdaw** pub opposite. (1 mile)

④ Facing the pub, turn right alongside the road. Immediately after passing a narrow lane and lodge house on the left, go left on a drive to **Denton Court** but after 200 yards go through a metal gate on the right and keep ahead towards a church, with a glimpse of the 16th century mansion through trees on the left.

Enter the churchyard; keep right of the 13th century church and go through the graveyard to a gap in the far right corner. Then turn right on a track to a gateway to the main road. Cross with care and go up **Snode Hill** opposite. Continue past the drive to **Tappington Hall Farm**; then go left along the next track, a little further uphill. You follow this track (which becomes an earth track) for 1½ miles, past cottages and, along the left edge of fields, under power lines and between fences, to pass a farm and reach a lane. (2½ miles)

⑤ Keep ahead along the lane opposite, with a line of beech and sycamore trees on the left, then 100 yards past a farm turn right on a track to **Ladwood Farm Cottages**. Keep straight on to the right of a house, to go through a gateway and uphill on the left edge of a field. At the top, veer right in front of trees, then after 200 yards bend left past trees, with a fence and hedge on the left, to a stile at the corner of a wood. Continue along the left edge of the wood to a metal gate, then 20 yards on, turn left through another gate and a belt of trees and go straight across a field to a gate by trees. Keep ahead along the right edge of a field, then left on a tarmac drive to a road. (1¼ miles)

⑥ Turn right along the road, then right again at a T-junction. Where this road bends left, go straight on over a stile and down a field, keeping left of trees, to a stile in the corner. From here the route across a large field is not obvious – go straight ahead to the top of a rise in the field and then bear slightly diagonally right, aiming for the left-hand of three pylons partially hidden behind trees ahead (to the right of a pylon standing bare in a field). As you get closer, aim for a gate in the treeline ahead, go through it and along the right edge of a field, passing a pylon in a depression on the right and ignoring a stile on the right. Keep ahead over a stile in the corner of the field; go along the right edge of a field and ahead where the fence on the right ends, to reach a metal gate to a lane. Go across to a stile and ahead to another, then along the left edge of a field and straight on to a stile. From the meadow here, flower-filled in summer, there is a wonderful view over the village of **Elham** and the picturesque valley. Go slightly diagonally right down the steep slope to a stile and down a bank to a lane; then turn left to follow the lane back to **Elham church** and the square. (2 miles)

Elham has some lovely old buildings, including the black and white timbered Abbot's Fireside, dating from 1614. There are other medieval houses, some with Georgian frontages, and the church dates from around 1200.

 Date walk completed:

HYTHE, THE ROYAL MILITARY CANAL AND LYMPNE

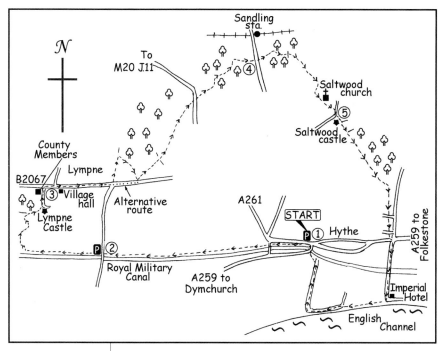

Distance:
9½ miles

Map: OS Explorer 138 Dover, Folkestone & Hythe

Starting Point:
The pay and display car park off Military Road in Hythe, GR 158347. Alternatively use the free car park at West Hythe, GR 125343, and start the walk at point 2.

How to get there: *From junction 11 of the M20, take the A261 into Hythe, with the car park on the left off Military Road, near the En Route tourist information office. The walk could be joined from Sandling Station on the Ashford to Folkestone line, ⅓ mile from point 4.*

THE COUNTY MEMBERS AT LYMPNE

*T*his route takes you through a variety of landscapes, each with its own fascination. You start at the historic town of Hythe, one of the original Cinque Ports. Though no longer a port, it has several interesting buildings, including the prominent church. You glimpse the famous miniature steam railway before walking alongside the Royal Military Canal, constructed in 1804–9 to repel Napoleon and now providing a tranquil water home for swans, coot and water lilies. Later you pass the ruins of a Roman fort, may be startled by the sounds of exotic animals, and can view Lympne Castle and church perched on the old cliffline, from which there are magnificent views over Romney Marsh. From Lympne village and pub you walk through woodland, alongside the route of a disused railway, and past ancient Saltwood Castle before finishing with a bracing stretch beside the sea and back to Hythe, where there is a wide choice of pubs, teashops and restaurants.

The unusually named **County Members** at **Lympne**, just over a third of the way round the walk, serves a good choice of ales, among them Greene King IPA, Badger Brewery's Fursty Ferret, Fuller's London Pride, and Watney's Best Mild. Food can be eaten in the roomy bar areas or in the pleasant conservatory and ranges from sandwiches, ploughman's and baguettes to lighter meals such as steak and ale pie and lamb moussaka and imaginative fare like breast of duck panfried with apple and honey sauce or guinea fowl with creamy Madeira and mushroom sauce.

Telephone: *01303 264759.*

① From the entrance to the car park, cross the busy road with care and turn right past the **En Route tourist information office** and on a path between the road and the tree-lined **Royal Military Canal**. At an information board just before a road junction go left to cross a road and go along **Green Lane** opposite. The canal is on your left, with the terminus of the **Romney, Hythe and Dymchurch Railway** beyond it, from where you may hear the miniature steam trains that run for 14 miles across **Romney Marsh**. You now walk alongside the canal for over 2 miles, either on the bank or the track below it, and can admire swans, water lilies, dragonflies in summer and perhaps even a kingfisher. Continue past a footbridge and straight across a road and through the small car park at **West Hythe**. (2¼ miles)

② After a further ½ mile alongside the canal, turn right at a marker post to cross a small footbridge over a stream and continue on a path between a hedge and a fence. The path climbs gradually up the slope of the old shoreline, with fine views to **Lympne Castle** and church on the ridge ahead. In the field on the right are the impressive walls of a Roman fortification from the 3rd century, now called **Stutfall Castle**, while to the left you may see or hear exotic animals, as these are compounds of **Port Lympne** animal park. The path finally goes up steps to reach a cross-path, where you turn right along the ridge, now on the **Saxon Shore Way** footpath. There are tremendous views across **Romney Marsh** to the coast, with **Dungeness** and **Hastings** in the distance. You curve left through trees to reach houses and a minor road. For a short diversion to view the castle and church, turn right for 300 yards and then retrace your steps.

Lympne Castle is really a fortified manor house, with a tower that dates back to the 13th century and a 14th century hall. The adjacent church has a Norman tower, built around 1100.

Otherwise, continue straight ahead along the road to a T-junction with a main road, with the **County Members** pub on the left. (1½ miles)

③ The walk continues by turning right at the T-junction, to go alongside the road past **Lympne village hall** and continue to where a road comes in from the right near a tall memorial. Here you can continue along the road, taking great care as there is no footpath, then go left at a stile by a gateway, 300 yards past **Oathill Cottages**, then right for a short distance to a marker on a gatepost. (To get to this point without road walking, go left on a footpath opposite the memorial to cross a field to a stile and go along the right edge of the next field to a stile in the corner. Over this, go back to the right to reach the corner of a wood and continue alongside it to a stile, then go diagonally right towards the stile and gateway to the road and left before them to the gatepost.) Continue diagonally left across a large field, aiming for the corner of a

THE IMPOSING WALLS OF SALTWOOD CASTLE ARE PASSED ON THE WAY

wood jutting out into the field on the left. Then maintain direction across the rest of the field to reach a cross-track. Go straight ahead on a sandy track curving left; then, when it bends right, go through the pedestrian gate ahead and diagonally right across a field to another gate in the far corner and onto a road. Cross with care on the corner to a track slightly to the left and go past a tiny church to a stile. Keep straight ahead across a field, keeping 20 yards left of a ditch and later the corner of a wood, to reach a gate into a wood. Stay on the main path as it bends between trees and go straight on at a marker post where a track leaves on the left, to continue past ancient oak trees and over a footbridge and curve right to a gate. Continue along the left edge of a field to a road. (2¼ miles)

④ Notice the lovely timbered cottage to the right here and go over the road to a footpath slightly to the left. The path crosses a footbridge and then goes between hedges and through trees. At a marker post at a major fork in the track near a large beech tree, go right on a sunken track, then at the next post keep ahead on the right-hand path and continue on the main track to reach a stile. Turn right on the cross-track beyond it, going straight over a farm track and downhill on a sandy track past orchards and plantations of Christmas trees, then large houses, to

a lane. Continue straight on, then, where the lane bends right, keep ahead through a gate and lychgate into the churchyard. Keep right of the ancient **Saltwood church**, well worth a look inside, to a gate at the end of the churchyard and go across a field to a metal gate between two barns and through the farmyard to a lane. (1 mile)

⑤ Turn right for 80 yards, then left after a lodge on a track to the left of a private road, taking you past **Saltwood Castle**.

In 1170 four assassins left Saltwood Castle for Canterbury, where they murdered the archbishop, Thomas à Becket, in the cathedral, an act which led to the city becoming the destination for pilgrims visiting Becket's tomb.

Keep straight on past (not under) a brick railway arch on the left, a reminder of the route of the dismantled **Hythe and Sandgate Railway**, which closed in 1951. Keep alongside trees on the former railway embankment on the left, then along the upper left edge of a field to a stile in the far left corner. Continue ahead on a track past a white house, then, after 100 yards, turn right down steps between gardens and go on a path that runs behind gardens to a road. Go straight across and down an alley, past an old millhouse and across a minor road to reach a

THE SUPERB VIEW ACROSS ROMNEY MARSH

main road near the **Bell** pub. (1 mile)

⑥ Cross with care to go down **Twiss Road** opposite. On reaching the **Royal Military Canal**, you can take a short-cut by turning right along the far bank and following it back to the **tourist information office** and the car park. For a pleasant seaside walk, continue ahead until you reach the promenade near the **Imperial Hotel** and turn right for ¾ mile. Just after passing a martello tower that has been converted into a house, bend right into **St Leonard's Road** and follow it back to the canal. Turn left to reach a main road by the **Duke's Head** pub and cross past the **tourist information office** to the car park. (1¾ miles)

Date walk completed:

FOLKESTONE WARREN, THE WHITE CLIFFS AND ALKHAM

THE MARQUIS OF GRANBY IN THE VILLAGE OF ALKHAM

Distance:
10¼ miles

Map: OS Explorer 138 Dover, Folkestone & Hythe

Starting Point:
The free car park
at East Cliff
Pavilion,
GR 239364, or the
pay and display
overflow car park
(summer only) just
north of it.

How to get there: *From junction 13 of the M20 follow
the signs to The Warren Country Park, then go down
Wear Bay Road to the East Cliff Pavilion.*

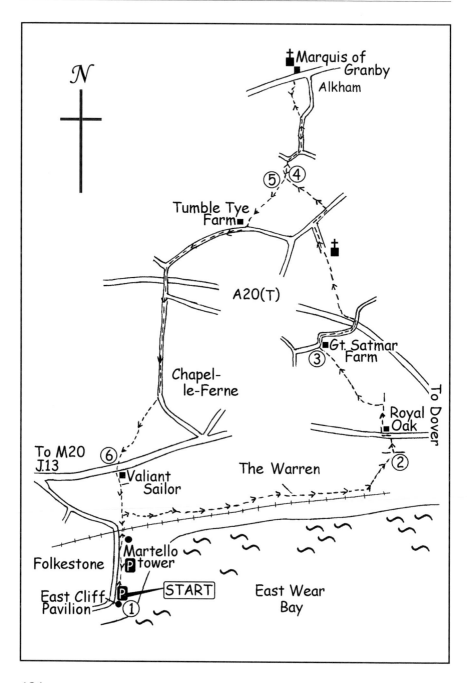

You start with a view over the harbour at Folkestone and walk through The Warren, beneath towering white cliffs and through luxuriant vegetation where rare insects and plants occur and migrant birds make landfall. After ascending the cliffs, with wonderful views over the English Channel to France, the route goes inland for a pub stop at Alkham, a lovely village nestling in a valley through the downs. You return to Folkestone via lanes and field paths, going back down the cliffs with more far-reaching views over the town to Romney Marsh and beyond. This walk requires a reasonable level of fitness, as it includes a strenuous climb up a long flight of steps cut into the cliff.

The **Marquis of Granby** is in a lovely position, nestling below the church in the village of **Alkham**, 6 miles from the start of the walk. The building, dating from 1810, has pleasant bar areas and a beamed restaurant inside, plus a garden. The emphasis is on fish, often cooked in a special recipe batter and including Dover or lemon sole and sea bass. You could tackle the fisherman's platter of scampi, plaice, scallops and haddock, but remember that you have to walk up a hill afterwards! There are also sandwiches, hot and cold baguettes, jacket potatoes, ploughman's and children's and vegetarian meals and a good choice of ales such as Ruddles County, Adnams Broadside and Morland Old Speckled Hen.

Telephone: *01304 822945.*

The Walk

① From the car park walk uphill alongside the road, past the mini-golf course and tennis courts, to another car park. Where it ends go right on a tarmac track, past a martello tower and straight ahead on a concrete path alongside a wooden fence. Just before a footbridge go right down steps to a tarmac road and turn right towards a caravan site, but before the first caravan on the right turn right down steps with a wooden hand-rail. The walk now goes for over 2 miles through **Folkestone Warren**, designated a Site of Special Scientific Interest because of its unique wildlife. Keep straight on at a marker post and go down more steps in the path; then continue along the main path to reach a railway. Continue alongside the railway, past buddleia bushes whose flowers in late summer provide welcome food for red admiral, painted lady and clouded yellow butterflies that have flown in from the Continent. Walk through a valley with rather primeval-looking vegetation, including a luxuriant carpet of hart's-tongue ferns, and keep straight on at a marker post. You re-emerge from the trees above the railway, with a tremendous view back to **Folkestone** and over the **English Channel** to France. Keep straight ahead past (not over) a footbridge over the railway, first alongside a wire fence then on a narrow path through chalk grassland, colourful with wild flowers and blue butterflies in season. To the left are towering white cliffs and you now ascend these cliffs up a long series of steps, stopping occasionally to admire the glorious views over the bay. (3 miles)

The distinctive landscape of Folkestone Warren is the result of some spectacular landslips, as the sea eroded the soft clay layer beneath the chalk. The area is home to over 150 species of birds and some rare moths, while plants such as rock sea lavender and wild

FOLKESTONE WARREN AND EAST WEAR BAY

cabbage occur on the cliffs. This unique ecology is now under conservation management by the White Cliffs Countryside Project.

② At the top of the cliffs, go right for 10 yards past a welcome seat and then left over a stile and alongside a caravan park to a road. Turn left and cross the road; then go ahead past the front of the **Royal Oak** pub, through wooden gates and left of a long building to a stile. Continue along the left edge of a field to another stile, then slightly diagonally right for 100 yards to a marker post. Turn left to a concrete road and left for 10 yards over a cattle grid, then right on a concrete track to the right of a bungalow. Keep right at a fork in the track to continue past static caravans, and where the concrete ends keep ahead across a large field, aiming towards a white house in trees to the left of grain silos. On the OS map the right of way goes to a stile and past the silos to a lane, but when I did the walk the obvious worn path through the crop reached the lane at a gap in the hedge to the left of **Great Satmar Farm**. (¾ mile)

③ Turn right along the lane from here and bend right on it when another lane goes straight on. The lane bends left on a bridge over a busy dual carriageway. Once across, turn immediately left at a bridleway sign, to go parallel with the main road for 100 yards to a gate, then diagonally right on a grassy path across a field towards a church. Keep left of the wall around the churchyard of the remote flint-built church of **Capel-le-Ferne**, which dates back to Norman times and is now under the care of the Churches Restoration Trust. Go through a gate and ahead on a tarmac track, then a lane, to a T-junction. Turn right for 300 yards and then left through a gap in the hedge at a bridleway sign. The path goes along the left edge of a field to a pylon and continues straight ahead. (1¼ miles)

④ On reaching a line of trees, you can continue to the pub at **Alkham**, in its lovely valley, before returning to this point (a return journey of 2 miles). If you don't wish to do this, go over the stile in the fence on the left, 10 yards before the trees, then follow the instructions from point 5. For the pub, go right through a metal gate to a path under the trees and leading to a lane. Turn right for 100 yards, then fork left and go ahead on another lane, soon going downhill. Just before a right bend, turn left opposite a wooden gate to go into trees and past a concrete footpath sign to a stile. Continue downhill towards a church nestling in trees in a picturesque valley, and over stiles and between gardens to an estate road. Turn right for 100 yards, then go left on a path between hedges to a road, with the **Marquis of Granby** pub at **Alkham** opposite. From the pub retrace your steps through the small estate and up the field to the lane. Turn right. Fork right at the junction, then right on a lane for 100 yards and left on the bridleway under trees to the metal gate. Go left for 10 yards to a stile in the fence opposite. (2 miles)

⑤ Go slightly diagonally left across the field, aiming slightly left of a pylon, to cross a stile. Turn sharp right immediately along the right edge of a field, walking alongside a fence to a stile onto a lane. Turn right along the lane, after ½ mile going past a large house to reach a T-junction. Go left, to soon cross a bridge back over the busy main road, and keep straight on where a lane goes off left. Continue on the lane for a further ¾ mile, going past a farm and uphill; then, as it bends left, go diagonally right on a track alongside a hedge. Keep straight across a field, beneath telegraph wires, then along the left side of a field, behind gardens and left through a gateway to a road opposite the **Valiant Sailor** pub. (2¼ miles)

⑥ Cross with care to a footpath to the right of the pub and continue ahead to a marker post at the end of gardens on the left. Go diagonally right at the post to walk downhill, soon with views over **Folkestone Harbour** and across the town to **Dungeness** and the downs near **Hastings** in the distance. Cross a footbridge over a road and continue ahead, to the right of the martello tower, and alongside the road back to the car park. If you wish to find out more about the history and natural history of the area, there is an information centre in the white martello tower behind the **East Cliff Pavilion**. (1 mile)

These martello towers are part of a chain of 74 that stretched from Folkestone to Seaford, west of Eastbourne. They were built in the early 19th century to defend the coast against an invasion by the French troops of Napoleon and were well equipped for the purpose, having walls 13 feet thick on the seaward side and a 2½ ton cannon that could fire a mile out to sea.

Date walk completed: